EMPOWERED MILLENNIAL INVESTOR

MICHAEL A. PAWLOWSKY, BCOM

DISCLAIMER

The information contained in this book is the opinion of the author and should not be considered professional financial advice. Please consult a financial professional before making any major financial decisions.

CONTENTS

EMPOWERED MILLENNIAL INVESTOR

INTRODUCTION

WHAT THIS BOOK IS NOT ABOUT

This book will not describe get-rich-quick schemes or help you identify the next "hot" stock that will make you rich. People who have insights into new technologies and emerging trends can see tremendous gains in their investment portfolios. For example, if you had invested $1,000 in shares of Apple in 2006, your investment would be worth nearly $38,000 almost 15 years later. Hindsight is 20/20 and if you are able to spot the next big trend and don't mind taking a risk, then go for it. Just be aware that even the best analysts on Wall Street can't predict the future and it is certainly beyond the scope of this book.

Investing in stocks for quick financial gain has its allure. The "fast money" approach has been glamorized in the media, but most people who invest for such short term gains almost always lose in the long run. These individuals may have a good idea for an investment, but once their investment does not produce the immediate gains they were hoping for, they often sell it at a loss and try to catch the next big upswing in another stock. This is not a sustainable approach to building wealth, as it relies mostly on chance.

WHAT THIS BOOK IS ABOUT

This book serves as a starting point for Canadian investors with little or no knowledge of taxes, retirement pensions or investments. It will give the novice investor knowledge, tools and actionable ideas in order to systematically build wealth over time to retire comfortably.

You will:

✓ Understand the basics of the Canadian income tax system.
✓ Know how much to expect (or not) from government pensions in retirement.
✓ Determine which registered savings vehicle such as an RRSP or TFSA (or both) is right for you.
✓ Evaluate the various investment options available to you.
✓ Make a plan to reach your investment goals.

"GENERATION SCREWED?"

Financial independence is a fantasy for most Canadians, especially younger Canadian belonging to the millennial generation (those born between 1981-1996) and Generation Z (those born after 1997). The media routinely mentions the financial plight of both these generations and how it may be the first time in Canadian history, perhaps with the exception of the Great Depression, that current generations may be worse off financially than their parents. Burdened with soaring student debt and bleak job prospects, many younger Canadians are entering the workforce with undergraduate and graduate degrees only to find work at a local coffee shop for close to minimum wage.

In fact, in 2013, the CBC aired a segment on *"The National"* that labeled the millennial generation "Generation Screwed".

The uncertainty of the economy, jobs and pensions is forcing many seniors back into the workforce, not because they want to work, but because of the inadequacy of their savings and pensions. With most people living longer, healthier lives, many seniors are forced to re-enter the workforce after their retirement to in order to supplement their incomes. This is tragic.

For most seniors, the amount received from public government pensions (Old Age Security and Canada Pension Plan) are inadequate for comfortable retirement living. With companies eliminating or reducing workplace pensions, the era of reliable pensions is coming to an end. Younger Canadians are increasingly choosing to work at various careers, industries and companies where most will not have a workplace pension to provide them with income in retirement. This shift is forcing younger Canadian to save for their own retirement, but with the public education system providing limited financial education, many have no idea where to start.

Younger Canadians are faced with challenges that our previous generations could never have imagined. They are the most educated, underemployed and indebted generation in Canadian history. Canadian millennials have lived through the 2008 financial crisis and along with Generation Z, have also lived through the global COVID-19 pandemic. Both generations have experienced the economic landscape shifting beneath their feet, but the members of those generations are also able to leverage their advanced knowledge of technology to empower themselves and adapt to new circumstances in order to succeed.

MY JOURNEY TO EMPOWERMENT

As a young millennial studying commerce at McGill University, the so called "Great Recession" of 2008 had a huge impact on me. Although I was still in school, witnessing the economy on the brink of collapse had its effect. I wondered about my own job prospects and after seeing thousands of people worldwide laid off from their jobs and evicted from their homes, I knew that nothing was certain. I vowed never to rely on the government or my employer to completely provide for my financial needs in retirement and decided to assert my own financial independence.

My own passion for investing began well before 2008. From a young age I started to educate myself and soaked up everything I could. I watched the business channel, followed the moving numbers at the bottom of the screen and listened to what guests and anchors were saying. At first, most of it appeared gibberish to me. However, I took an active interest and slowly the language of investing started making sense.

The public education system did a great job teaching us how to write an essay and solve for 'X', but when it came to understanding where the money goes that comes off our paycheck, no one seemed to know. I thought that would change at university when I actually started specializing in commerce, but it didn't. The professor of my Investments and Portfolio Management class had a PhD in Finance, but had never bought a share of stock in his whole life. I learned theories and concepts, but no concrete ways to take action and start investing.

My formal studies provided an excellent foundation for understanding financial concepts, but my real financial education came from outside the classroom by reading books, investing small amounts and learning from my mistakes.

I now have the confidence to manage my own investments, and feel secure that I will live retirement on my own terms. It is my goal to impart this knowledge to you, so you become empowered to better understand taxes, retirement and investing.

BRAVE NEW WORLD

Unfortunately for younger Canadians, current interest rates are considerably lower than in previous generations. Most savings accounts don't pay enough interest to keep up with inflation. Banking fees have also increased. Putting it all together means that keeping money in a bank account results in a decrease in wealth over time. With interest rates so low, many younger Canadians have turned don't know how to even begin to invest for the long term.

I always wanted to help people with their finances and thought that a career as a financial advisor would be a great way to combine my passion for investing and helping others. One of my courses at McGill University required that I interview someone in my chosen career path so I interviewed my family's financial advisor.

I assumed that a financial advisor was someone who actively managed investments, had advanced knowledge of financial markets and put their client's needs first. Was I wrong! My family's financial advisor spoke almost exclusively about "sales quotas" and "financial products" such as mutual funds. Most financial advisors' compensation has nothing to do with how your investments perform. Rather they are paid depending on the number of new clients they bring to the firm and the amount of "products" they are able to sell. It is a fundamental misalignment of interests. Many financial advisors are looking after themselves, not you.

The prevailing wisdom of our parents' generation when it came to investing was to seek the advice of the financial advisor at one's local bank, buy diversified mutual funds and contribute to a Registered Retirement Savings Plan (RRSP). This may have been good advice at the time, but many things have changed. Most notably, the availability of free information on the internet, lower cost alternatives to mutual funds known as Exchange Traded Funds (ETFs) and a new type of savings vehicle known as a Tax-Free Savings Account (TFSA).

STRUCTURE OF THE BOOK

Part 1 explores at a basic level how the Canadian taxation system works and how different types of income are taxed. It might not be readily apparent, but taxation plays a crucial role in determining your real investment returns.

Part 2 reviews government pensions that Canadians can expect in retirement, (Canada Pension Plan and Old Age Security) so you can get a sense how much retirement income you can expect from these pensions.

Part 3 evaluates the advantages and disadvantages of the two main savings vehicles: Registered Retirement Savings Plans (RRSPs) and Tax-Free Savings Accounts (TFSAs).

Part 4 examines investment options: savings accounts, Guaranteed Investment Certificates (GICs), stocks, income trusts, mutual funds, and Exchange Traded Funds (ETFs).

Part 5 provides an overview of setting a goal to reach retirement and making a plan to reach that goal. There are various ways to do that such as using a financial advisor, managing your own portfolio or using an all-in-one portfolio.

All the terms in italics can be found in the glossary at the back of the book.

EMPOWER YOURSELF

Despite the challenges that young Canadians face, the future is bright for those who understand how the financial landscape has changed and what they can do to adapt and thrive. Starting today, you can take immediate action to ensure that you take the steps to live retirement on your own terms.

By reading this book you will learn the language of personal finance, keep more of your money in your pocket and make a plan that works for you to reach your retirement goals.

You will learn what the financial services industry doesn't want you to know: how small fees can add up to a fortune over time.

You will learn the small steps you can take, such as automatically setting aside a percentage of your income and investing it to take advantage of compounded returns.

The best investment you can make is in your own personal financial education. By continuously educating yourself, you will be empowered to take your financial future into your own hands with confidence. Congratulations on taking the first step.

PART 1: TAXATION

Before exploring the different types of investments, it is of paramount importance to understand on a basic level how the Canadian income tax system works.

A large part of your investment return is dependent on how your income is taxed. Depending on where in Canada you live, the type of income you receive, and the type of account you receive it in, will all make a difference in the amount of tax that you will have to pay.

Every successful investor must have a least a basic understanding of how their income is taxed. Prior to making any investment, it is important to understand how your potential gains will be taxed. After all, it is the money that stays in your pocket that is the real return on your investment.

This part of the book focuses on how employment income and investment income (dividend, interest, and capital gain income) are taxed differently. It will also explore some of the most commonly available tax credits.

EMPLOYMENT INCOME

Employment income is the income you receive for being employed. For the vast majority of people in Canada, especially the millennial generation, this is the main source of taxable income.

In Canada, income taxes are paid to both the federal government and depending on where you reside, the provincial or territorial government.

Federal income tax rates are the same for all Canadians, while provincial and territorial income tax rates can differ greatly. Like many other countries, Canada and its provinces and territories use a progressive system of tax brackets. In other words, the more money you make, the more tax you will have to pay once your income exceeds a certain threshold.

Under a progressive system, if you earn $80,000 of employment income, you will pay a 15% federal tax on the first $48,535 and 20.5% on the remaining income that exceeds $48,535 up to the next income tax bracket. You will not have to pay 20.5% federal income tax on your entire income, only the amount that exceeds that first income tax bracket.

Federal tax rates are the same for all Canadians regardless of where you live – see Table 1. Provincial and territorial rates can differ quite greatly – see Table 2.

Your *marginal (tax) rate* is the rate you pay on one additional dollar of earnings. Put another way, you will be taxed at a rate of 15% for every dollar you earn up to $48,535. Should you exceed $48,535, your federal marginal tax rate will be 20.5% up to the next tax bracket.

For example, if you earned $50,000 your federal marginal tax rate would be 20.5% because every dollar you earn that exceeds the first tax bracket ($48,535) will be taxed at 20.5% up to the next tax bracket. Every dollar you earned up to $48,535 will still be taxed at a rate of 15%.

For the latest rates visit the Canada Revenue Agency website at www.cra-arc.gc.ca

Table 1 - 2020 Federal Income Tax Rates

Country	Rate(s) on *taxable* income
Canada	15.0% on the first $48,535 + 20.5% on the next $48,534 + 26.0% on the next $53,404+ 29.0% on the next $63,89+ 33.0% of taxable income over $214,368

Table 2 - 2020 Provincial Income Tax Rates

Provinces / Territories	Rate(s) on *taxable* income
Yukon	6.4% on the first $48,535+ 9.0% on the next $48,535+ 10.9% on the next $53,404 + 12.8% on the next $349,527+ 15.0% on the amount over $500,000
Northwest Territories	5.9% on the first $43,957 + 8.6% on the next $43,959 + 12.2% on the next $55,016 + 14.05% on the amount over $142,932
Nunavut	4.0% on the first $46,277 + 7.0% on the next $46,278 + 9.0% on the next $57,918 + 11.5% on the amount over $150,473
Newfoundland Labrador	8.7% on the first $37,929+ 14.5% on the next $37,929 + 15.8% on the next $59,574+ 17.3% on the next $54,172+ 18.3% on the amount over $189,604
Prince Edward Island	9.8% on the first $31,984 + 13.8% on the next $31,985 + 16.7% on the amount over $63,969
Nova Scotia	8.79% on the first $29,590 + 14.95% on the next $29,590 + 16.67% on the next $33,820 +

Provinces / Territories	Rate(s) on *taxable* income
	17.5% on the next $57,000 +
	21.0% on the amount over $150,000
New Brunswick	9.68% on the first $43,401 +
	14.82% on the next $43,402 +
	16.52% on the next $54,319 +
	17.84% on the next $19,654+
	20.3% on the amount over $160,776
Quebec	15.0% on the first $43,790 +
	20.0% on the next $43,790 +
	24.0% on the next $18,980 +
	25.75% on the amount over $106,555
Manitoba	10.8% on the first $33,389 +
	12.75% on the next $38,775 +
	17.4% on the amount over $72,164
Alberta	10.0% on the first $131,220+
	12.0% on the next $26,244+
	13.0% on the next $52,488 +
	14.0% on the next $104,976+
	15.0% on the amount over $314,928
Ontario	5.05% on the first $44,740 +
	9.15% on the next $44,742 +
	11.16% on the next $60,518 +
	12.16% on the next $70,000 +
	13.16 % on the amount over $220,000
Saskatchewan	10.5% on the first $45,225 +
	12.5% on the next $83,989 +
	14.5% on the amount over $129,214
British Columbia	5.06% on the first $41,725 +
	7.7% on the next $41,726 +
	10.5% on the next $12,361 +
	12.29% on the next $20,532 +
	14.7% on the next $41,404 +
	16.8% on the amount over $157,748

Federal Income Tax on Employment Income

Here is a simple example demonstrating how federal income tax is calculated on employment income assuming you earn $30,000.

The $30,000 would be taxed according to the federal tax rates for that year. Let's use the federal tax rates shown in Table 1.

The first $30,000 of income is taxed at 15% (your marginal federal tax rate).

Income Tax: $30,000 x 15.0% =	$4,500.00

The federal tax you owe before any applicable tax credits is **$4,500.**

Federal Tax Credits

There are two types of tax credits, refundable and non-refundable. A refundable credit is a credit that can be paid to you even if you do not have any taxable income. A non-refundable tax credit only serves to reduce your total income tax owed and no direct payment will be made to you. With the passing of each federal budget each spring, the government may introduce or remove various tax credits. For example, for a number of years, taxpayers used to be able to claim a tax credit for the cost of public transit passes, however this tax credit was removed in 2017.

Although you initially owe $4,500, as an employed worker, you are eligible for certain federal non-refundable tax credits that will reduce your overall federal tax owed.

Some of the most common federal non-refundable tax credits that you may be eligible for are (just to name a few) are:

- Basic Personal Amount
- Canada Pension Plan Contributions
- Employment Insurance Premiums

- Canada Employment Amount

Each of these provides a tax credit at a rate of 15% (lowest federal bracket). Let's look at them one by one.

The Basic Personal Amount

The basic personal amount is a federal non-refundable tax credit that is available to everyone who files a tax return and is equal to 15% of the basic personal amount.

In December 2019, some changes were announced to how the basic personal amount is calculated. Beginning in 2020, the maximum basic personal amount was increased from $12,298 in 2019 to $13,229 in 2020 for individuals with a net income of $150,473 or less. The increase is gradually reduced for individuals with net income between $150,473 and $214,368. For example, if your net income is above $214,368, the change does not apply to you and your basic personal amount will be $12,298.

In addition, the maximum basic personal amount will be increased to $15,000 by 2023 as follows:

$13,808 for the 2021 taxation year,

$14,398 for the 2022 taxation year, and

$15,000 for the 2023 taxation year, and indexed for inflation for subsequent years.

Individuals whose net income is too high to benefit from the increased basic personal amount will continue to claim the existing basic personal amount. This existing amount will continue to be indexed for inflation each year.

In 2020, the basic personal amount was $13,229 and 15% of that is **$1,984.35**.

This $1,984.35 credit will be deducted from the taxes that you owe ($4,500).

As this is a non-refundable tax credit, if you did not have any income you would not receive a check for $1,984.35, as it can only reduce the income tax to a maximum of the taxes owed.

Canada Pension Plan (CPP) or Quebec Pension Plan (QPP) Contributions

The amount an employee contributes to the Canada Pension Plan (CPP) or the Quebec Pension Plan (QPP) is also eligible for a federal non-refundable tax credit.

Later, we will go into more detail regarding the CPP and QPP. For now, just know that virtually all employees over the age of 18 in Canada who earn more than $3,500 of employment income annually must contribute to the CPP or QPP.

If you are an employee the province of Quebec you must contribute to the QPP and if you are an employee anywhere else in Canada you must contribute to the CPP. Both plans require the employee and their employer to make matching contributions that amount to approximately 10% of the employee's pay, up to a maximum contribution amount.

Contributions deducted from each paycheck are invested by the pension plan. The maximum amount an employee could contribute in 2020 to the CPP was $2,898.00 (the employer will also contribute $2,898.00) based on a salary of up to a maximum $58,700. Please note however that only the employee portion of contributions is eligible for the tax credit.

Based on a $30,000 salary, you contribute approximately $1,400 to the CPP and your employer matches that contribution. The non-refundable tax credit amount is 15% of the amount of employee CPP contributions which is: 15% x $1,400 = $210. As a federal non-refundable tax credit, it reduces your federal income tax owed by **$210**.

Employment Insurance (EI) Premiums

The amount an employee pays in Employment Insurance (EI) premiums is also eligible for a non-refundable tax credit.

The Employment Insurance program is mandatory for all Canadian workers regardless of age and is automatically deducted from your paycheck up to a maximum amount each year. It is designed to provide temporary income to unemployed Canadians who have lost their job through no fault of their own. More information about what benefits are available to EI recipients can be found at www.servicecanada.gc.ca.

In 2020, an employee had to pay $1.58 for every $100 in employment earnings. Based on a $30,000 salary, you would pay $474 in EI premiums. The non-refundable tax credit amount is 15% of this amount which is: 15% x $474 = $71.10. As a federal non-refundable tax credit, it reduces your federal income tax owed by **$71.10**.

The Canada Employment Amount

The Canada employment amount is a federal non-refundable tax credit available to all Canadian employees (except self-employed) in recognition of expenses that workers must incur such as uniforms and supplies in order to perform their work duties. The Canada employment amount is not dependent on income and is the same for everyone.

In 2020, the maximum amount that could be claimed was $1,245. The non-refundable tax credit amount is 15% of this amount which is: 15% x $1,245= $186.75. As a federal non-refundable tax credit, it can only reduce your federal income tax owed by **$186.75**.

***

For a quick review of the federal non-refundable tax credits you are eligible for:

Basic Personal Amount: $13,229 x 15.0% =	$1,984.35
CPP Contributions: $1,400 x 15.0% =	$210.00
EI Premiums: $474 x 15.0% =	$71.10
Canada Employment Amt. : $1,245 x 15.0% =	$186.75
Total Federal Non-Refundable Tax Credits =	**$2,452.20**

Then you can deduct this amount from your federal tax owed:

Federal Tax Owed Before Tax Credits =	$4,500.00
Total Non-Refundable Federal Tax Credits =	($2,452.20)
Net Federal Tax Owed After Tax Credits =	**$2,047.80**

Based on a $30,000 salary, before calculating the federal non-refundable tax credits, you owed the federal government $4,500. Once the federal non-refundable tax credits were calculated, it reduced your tax bill by $2,452.20 so the final amount that you owe to the federal government is **$2,047.80**.

Provincial Income Tax on Employment Income

Let's continue assuming you earn $30,000 in employment income. Now let's also say you are an Ontario resident.

The way that Ontario calculates provincial tax and non-refundable tax credits is very similar to the way federal income tax and non-refundable tax credits are calculated.

Let's quickly review the Ontario tax brackets from Table 2:

Ontario	
	5.05% on the first $44,740 +
	9.15% on the next $44,742 +
	11.16% on the next $60,518 +
	12.16% on the next $70,000 +
	13.16 % on the amount over $220,000

The first $30,000 of income is taxed at 5.05%. Your marginal provincial tax rate is 5.05%.

Income Tax : $30,000 x 5.05% =	$1,515.00

The provincial tax you owe before any applicable tax credits is **$1,515**.

Just like federal employment income taxation, although you owe $1,515.00, as an employee you are eligible for certain non-refundable tax credits that will reduce the overall provincial tax you owe. Let's assume the provincial non-refundable tax credits that you are eligible for are the:

- Basic Personal Amount
- Canada Pension Plan (CPP) Contributions
- Employment Insurance (EI) Premiums

Provincial Tax Credits

Ontario Basic Personal Amount

The Ontario basic personal amount is a non-refundable tax credit that is available to every Ontario resident who files a tax return and is equal to 5.05% of the basic personal amount.

In 2020, the basic personal amount was $10,783 and 5.05% of that is **$544.54**. As this is a non-refundable tax credit, if you did not have any income you would not receive a check for $544.54, as it can only reduce the provincial income tax to a maximum of the taxes owed.

CPP Contributions

Based on a $30,000 salary, you contribute $1,400 (approximately) to the CPP and your employer matches that contribution. The non-refundable tax credit amount is 5.05% of the amount of employee CPP contributions which is: 5.05% x $1,400 = $70.70 and will reduce your provincial taxes owed by **$70.70**.

EI Premiums

Based on a $30,000 salary, you would pay $474 in EI premiums. The non-refundable tax credit amount is 5.05% of the amount of the premiums paid to EI, which is 5.05% x $474 = $23.94 and reduce your provincial taxes owed by **$23.94**.

***

Here is a review of the non-refundable provincial tax credits:

Basic Personal Amount: $10,783 x 5.05% =	$544.54
CPP Contributions: $1,200 x 5.05% =	$70.70
EI Premiums: $565 x 5.05% =	$23.94
Total Prov. Non-Refundable Tax Credits =	**$639.18**

Then you can deduct this amount from your provincial tax owed:

Provincial Tax Owed Before Tax Credits =	$1,515.00
Total Non-Refundable Prov. Tax Credits =	($639.18)
Net Provincial Tax Owed After Tax Credits =	**$875.82**

Based on a $30,000 salary, before calculating the provincial non-refundable tax credits, you owed the provincial government $1,515. Once the provincial non-refundable tax credits were calculated, it reduced your taxes owed by $587.21 so the final amount that you owe to the provincial government is **$875.82**.

By adding the federal and provincial taxes owed, you obtain your total employment income tax:

Federal Tax Owed =	$2,047.80
Provincial Tax Owed =	$875.82
Total Employment Income Tax =	**$2,923.62**

INVESTMENT INCOME

Investment income is income that is earned from:

- Dividends paid by corporations

- Interest payments on a loan

- Capital gains earned from the sale of an asset

Now let's explore how dividends, interest and capital gains are taxed.

DIVIDEND INCOME

A *dividend* is paid to shareholders of a corporation as a portion of a corporation's profits. Once a corporation has paid all of its expenses, presumably it has a profit. It can either return the profit to shareholders in the form of a dividend, retain the profits in the corporation to grow earnings, or a combination of the two.

Generally, mature corporations that operate in stable industries pay out a significant portion of their earnings to shareholders in the form of a dividend, known as a payout ratio. For example, Bell Canada has a policy to payout between 65% - 75% of their earnings to shareholders in the form of a dividend and retain the rest to keep growing earnings. These policies are not set in stone and can change over time. In fact, some corporations eliminate their dividends altogether.

Less established corporations or corporations that operate in less stable industries usually do not pay a dividend because they want to retain any profits in the corporation to fuel the growth and expansion of the business.

When received by the shareholder, dividend income is taxed less than other forms of income because the corporation that paid the dividend has already paid tax on their earnings. In order to avoid or minimize this "double taxation", government taxation agencies use a confusing system of increasing taxable income and then offering a dividend tax credit.

Eligible Vs Non-Eligible Dividends

Canadian corporations can issue both "eligible" and "non-eligible" dividends, and the main difference is the way that they are taxed.

Eligible Dividends

The vast majority of Canadian corporations that trade on the Toronto Stock Exchange pay eligible dividends to shareholders. To understand their taxation, consider the following example:

Let's assume that your only source of income comes from eligible dividends that pay you $30,000 a year. As eligible dividends, they are subject to a "gross up" factor of 38%, so you would increase your dividend income by 38% in order to bring your income up to the approximate amount of income that the corporation has already paid tax on before applying the dividend tax credit.

Actual Dividend Income =	$30,000.00
"Grossed Up": $30,000 x 1.38 =	$41,400.00

At this stage, you may be thinking "why am I being charged tax on $41,400 when I only received $30,000?"

Stay tuned and let's see how this amount is taxed at the federal and provincial levels.

Federal Tax

At this stage, tax is calculated at your applicable marginal tax rate. Since this is your only source of income, you are in the lowest federal tax bracket of 15%.

Income Tax : $41,400 x 15% =	$6,210.00

Then, you would apply the federal dividend tax credit (15%) on the grossed up amount.

Fed. Dividend Tax Credit : $41,400 x 15% =	$6,210.00

Then you subtract the income tax owed from the dividend tax credit.

Federal Tax Owed : $6,210 – $6,210 =	**$0.00**

Although tax was calculated on the grossed up amount of $41,400, with the application of the dividend tax credit you end up paying absolutely no federal tax on your dividends.

Ontario Tax

In order to calculate the amount of provincial tax owed on your eligible dividends, the same process applies, although with a different marginal tax rate and dividend tax credit rate.

You would first gross up your dividend income by 38% and then calculate the tax owed at the applicable tax brackets.

Income Tax : $41,400 x 5.05% =	$2,090.70

Next, you would apply the provincial dividend tax credit (10%) on the grossed up amount.

Ont. Dividend Tax Credit = $41,400 x 10% =	$4,140.00

Finally, you subtract the income tax owed from the dividend tax credit.

Prov. Tax Owed = $2,110.30 – $4,140.00 =	**$0.00 ***

* Since the dividend tax credit is a non-refundable tax credit, taxes payable are simply reduced to $0, even though the amount of the credit exceeds the amount of taxes owed.

There is a tremendous tax benefit to income received from dividends and many wealthy individuals receive the majority of their income in the form of dividends in order to minimize the amount of taxes that they pay.

Non-Eligible Dividends

For non-eligible dividends paid by Canadian corporations the gross up factor is 25% and a federal dividend tax credit is calculated as 2/3 of the gross-up (or 13.3333% of the grossed-up dividends).

The gross up factor used by provincial and territorial governments differ, so check with your provincial or territorial taxation agency for the latest information.

Non-eligible dividends are paid by Canadian controlled private corporations, so if you own publicly traded shares of a Canadian corporation you will be receiving eligible dividends.

Foreign Corporation Dividends

Dividends received from foreign corporations are not eligible for any dividend tax credits. They are taxed at your marginal rate and depending on what country the corporation is based in, a withholding tax may be deducted at source. The withholding tax is deducted immediately when the dividend is paid and only the portion that you receive is taxed at your marginal rate. For example:

- If you hold shares of a U.S. based dividend paying corporation, 15% of your dividend will be withheld at payment by your broker. For example, if you received a $100 dividend payment from a U.S. corporation, you will only receive $85.

- Shares of U.S. based corporations held in a Registered Retirement Savings Plan (RRSP) or a Registered Retirement Income Fund (RRIF) are not subjected to a withholding tax.

Canada has tax treaties with many countries and you should consult the Canada Revenue Agency (CRA) website to determine what withholding taxes may apply to foreign dividends.

INTEREST INCOME

Interest is paid to lenders of money and is the cost associated with borrowing money.

Interest income is taxed at your marginal tax rate, just like employment income. For individuals, there are no tax credits to offset the amount of taxes you must pay for interest income, except for the basic personal amount (federal and provincial) which applies to all types of income.

Let's assume that your only source of income is interest income that pays you $30,000 a year. As interest income is taxed at your marginal tax rate, the federal rate would be 15% and the Ontario provincial rate would be 5.05%.

Fed. Tax Owed: $30,000 x 15% =	$4,500.00
Prov. Tax Owed: $30,000 x 5.05% =	$1,515.00
Total Tax Owed =	$6,015.00

You would then deduct the basic personal amount for both federal and provincial governments:

Federal: $13,229 x 15.0% =	$1,984.35
Provincial: $10,783 x 5.05%	$544.54
Total Basic Personal Amounts Credits =	$2,528.89

Taxes Owed: $6,015.00 – $2,528.89 =	**$3,486.11**

Unlike dividend income, there are very little tax advantages to receiving interest income.

More information on the taxation of interest and other investment income can be found at the CRA website.

CAPITAL GAINS

A *capital gain* is a profit earned when you sell an asset for more than you paid for it. Only 50% of a capital gain is taxable at your marginal rate. This applies to real estate (except your primary residence), stocks, bonds, income trusts, mutual funds and exchange traded funds (ETFs).

For example, assume you buy 500 shares of Apple stock at $100 each for a total investment of $50,000. One year later the price of your shares has increased to $160 each. You decide to sell your shares resulting in an increase of your original investment of $50,000 to $80,000 for a $30,000 capital gain.

The capital gain is calculated by subtracting the sale amount from the total amount that you paid for the shares.

Investment Amount: 500 shares x $100 =	$50,000.00
Sale Amount: 500 shares x $160 =	$80,000.00
Capital Gain: $80,000 - $50,000 =	$30,000.00

Your capital gain would be $30,000, but only half of the amount of the capital gain is taxable at your marginal tax rate.

Taxable Amount: $30,000 x 50% =	$15,000.00
Federal Tax: $15,000 x 15% =	$2,250.00
Provincial Tax: $15,000 x 5.05% =	$757.50
Taxes Owed: $2,250 + $757.50 =	$3,007.50

Then deduct the basic personal amounts for both federal and provincial governments to get the amount of tax owed:

Federal: $13,229 x 15.0% =	$1,984.35
Provincial: $10,783 x 5.05%	$544.54
Total Basic Personal Amounts Credits =	$2,528.89

Taxes Owed: $3,007.50 – $2,528.89 =	**$478.61**

The fact that half the capital gain is not taxable produces a great tax advantage compared to interest and employment income.

The opposite of a capital gain is a *capital loss* and occurs when an investor sells an investment for less than they paid for it. Capital losses can be used to offset any taxable capital gains in any of the three preceding years or in any future year. The full amount of the loss can be used to offset any eligible capital gains.

More information on taxation of capital gains and losses can be found at the CRA website.

A COMPARISON OF TAXATIONS

Table 3 compares the amount of tax owed for employment income and the three types of investment income (dividend, interest and capital gains) from the previous examples:

Table 3 - Taxation of $30,000 Earned from Different Sources

Source of Income	Tax on $30,000
Employment	$2,923.62
Dividend	$0
Interest	$3,486.11
Capital Gains	$478.61

Looking at Table 3, it is immediately apparent that dividend and capital gains income stand out as the lowest taxed forms of income.

In recent years, as the gap between rich and the poor has grown, many people are frustrated at the idea of wealthy individuals paying taxes at lower rates than most other people. How does it make sense that a millionaire pays a lower tax rate than a teacher or nurse?

Wealthy individuals understand taxation and are able to preserve and grow their wealth by receiving the majority of their income as investment income such as dividends and capital gains.

Now you know too.

By understanding the basics of how different incomes are taxed, you can empower yourself with the same knowledge that the wealthy use to keep more of their wealth and pay less tax.

For the vast majority of Canadian retirees, the federal government pensions (Canada Pension Plan and Old Age Security) make up the foundation of their retirement incomes. Before you decide what investment choices are right for you, it is important to first understand what you can expect to receive in the way of federal government pensions in retirement.

PART 2: FEDERAL GOVERNMENT PENSIONS

Most industrialized countries provide their senior citizens with income security in retirement in the form of a state pension. Canada is no exception as Canadians have two federal government administered pension plans: Old Age Security and the Canada Pension Plan/Quebec Pension Plan.

The first such pension, the Old Age Security pension, was first introduced in 1951 to establish a universal pension plan for Canadians. In 1965, to further enhance income security for Canadian workers in retirement, a mandatory contribution based pension plan known as the Canada Pension Plan was introduced.

Both these pensions were created as income security safety nets for seniors in retirement and were never meant to provide for all of a senior's income needs in retirement.

OLD AGE SECURITY (OAS)

OAS is a monthly pension that is payable to most Canadian residents over the age of 65.

Canadian residents are eligible to receive the OAS pension based on their age, legal status in Canada and years of residency. Currently, you must be 65 years of age, be a Canadian citizen or legal resident and have resided in Canada for at least 10 years after the age of 18.

In January 2021, the maximum OAS monthly benefit was $615.37 in you choose to start your pension at 65. The benefit is adjusted quarterly to keep pace with inflation. In order to receive the maximum OAS pension you must have lived in Canada for 40 years after the age of 18.

If you lived in Canada between 10 and 40 years, your pension will be reduced according to the years of residency in Canada. For example, if you have only lived 10 years in Canada and you would like to receive your OAS pension at age 65, your benefit would be ¼ of the maximum amount (10 years out of 40) and your monthly OAS benefit would be $153.84 ($615.37 x ¼) per month.

You can delay receiving your pension in order to qualify for, or increase your monthly benefit if you do not have sufficient years of residency. Depending on what other countries you have lived in, you may be able to receive a higher monthly amount if Canada has an international agreement with that country.

For more information on the OAS please visit the Service Canada website: http://www.servicecanada.gc.ca

The amount of the OAS benefit that you receive also depends on your net income. When you become eligible for the OAS pension, an important consideration is that depending on your annual income, all or part of your pension must be paid back to the government. This is commonly referred to as the 'Claw Back' but officially known as the 'Recovery Tax'.

If your net income exceeded $77,580 in the 2019 taxation year, then you would have to pay back a portion (15%) of the income that exceeds the threshold on a monthly basis.

If your income exceeds $117,954 in 2015, you would be subject to a full recovery of the OAS pension and not receive any OAS payments.

For example, if your net income for 2019 is $85,000, you would have to pay back 15% of the amount exceeding $77,580 (the minimum income recovery threshold):

Exceeding Threshold: $85,000 - $77,580 =	$7,420.00
Recovery Tax: $7,420.00 x 15% =	$1,113.00

The repayment amount ($1,078.65) is divided monthly and deducted from your OAS payments as a recovery tax the following year.

Monthly Recovery Tax: $1,113.00/ 12 =	$92.75

So your monthly benefit would be reduced by $92.75 from July 2020 – June 2021.

Should your income in subsequent years decline below the threshold, then you would no longer be subject to the recovery tax. The recovery tax is re-evaluated annually when you file your income tax return.

For more information on the OAS recovery tax please visit the Service Canada website.

Related to the OAS are additional benefits for seniors with low income. These benefits are not taxable at the federal and provincial/territorial levels and include the Guaranteed Income Supplement (GIS), the Allowance, and the Allowance for the Survivor.

Guaranteed Income Supplement (GIS)

The GIS provides a monthly non-taxable supplement to people receiving OAS whose income falls below a certain threshold. Just like OAS, the GIS is adjusted quarterly to protect against inflation.

The amount that you are eligible to receive depends on your income and marital status. The figures below represent the maximum annual income threshold to receive any GIS payment. The higher your reported income, the less GIS you would be eligible to receive and vice versa. The maximum annual income threshold does not include OAS payments. In other words, the amount you receive from OAS is not counted as part of your annual income. See Table 4 below for more details. The figures are current as of January 2021.

Table 4 - Maximum Annual Income Threshold to Receive the GIS

Marital Status	Maximum Annual Income
If you are a single, widowed or divorced pensioner	$18,648 (individual income)
If your spouse/common-law partner receives the full OAS pension	$24,624 (combined income)
If your spouse/common-law partner does not receive an OAS pension	$44,688 (combined income)
If your spouse/common-law partner receives the Allowance	$44,688 (combined income)

The Allowance and the Allowance for the Survivor

For eligible spouses or common-law partners aged 60-64, another benefit is available known as the Allowance. The Allowance is for spouses or common law partners of someone receiving the OAS pension who are aged 60-64 and whose combined income falls below a certain threshold. The Allowance for the Survivor is intended for people aged 60-64 whose spouse or common law partner has deceased.

See the table below for more details on the Allowance, and Allowance for the Survivor. The actual amount of the Allowance or the Allowance for the Survivor, depends on your reported income.

Table 5 below shows the maximum annual income threshold to receive any Allowance or Allowance for the Survivor payment. The higher your reported income, the less Allowance or Allowance for the Survivor you would be eligible to receive and vice versa. The figures are current as of January 2021.

Table 5 - Maximum Income Threshold to Receive the Allowance and Allowance for the Survivor

	Maximum Annual Income
Allowance	$34,512 (combined income)
Allowance for the Survivor	$25,152 (individual income)

More information on the GIS, the Allowance, and the Allowance for the Survivor payment amounts can be found at the Service Canada website.

CANADA AND QUEBEC PENSION PLANS

The Canada Pension Plan (CPP) was first established in 1965 as a way to force Canadian employees to save for retirement. The plan is mandatory for employees in Canada (except Quebec - more on this below) over the age of 18 who are not already receiving the pension regardless of citizenship. The CPP is a monthly retirement benefit that is annually adjusted to keep pace with inflation. Enrollment in the CPP is automatic and you can see the amount of your contributions that are deducted on your pay stub.

Up until 2019, the CPP retirement pension replaced 25% of your average employment earnings up to a maximum earnings limit each year with the first $3,500 of employment earning being exempt from CPP contributions.

Beginning in 2019, the CPP enhancement means that the CPP will begin to grow to replace 33% of the average work earnings you receive after 2019. The maximum limit used to determine your average employment earnings will also gradually increase by 14% by 2025.

For example, in 2019, both the employee and the employer contribute to the plan for a total contribution of 10.2% of the employee's salary with both the employer and employee contributing equal amounts (employee: 5.1%, employer: 5.1%). Self-employed workers must also contribute to the CPP, except that they must contribute the full 10.2%. The percentage that the employee and employer contribute will also increase each year through 2023 up to the maximum earnings limit.

Furthermore, beginning in 2024, a second, higher maximum earnings limit will be introduced, known as the second earnings ceiling, that may require you and your employer to contribute an additional portion of your earnings to the CPP. This new limit, known as the year's additional maximum pensionable earnings, will not replace the first earnings ceiling. Instead, it will subject your earnings to two earnings limits. For example, this new range of earnings covered by the CPP will start at the first earnings ceiling (estimated to be $69,700 in 2025) and go to the second earnings ceiling which will be 14% higher by 2025 (estimated to be $79,400).

Contributions to the CPP must be made from employment income, so any other forms of income are not subjected to the requirement of making CPP contributions. In 2019, the maximum annual pensionable earnings limit was $57,400. Since the first $3,500 is exempt from CPP contribution, the maximum contributory earnings was $53,900.00. In 2019, at an employee contribution rate of 5.10%, the maximum annual employee contribution was $2,748.90.

Contributions are invested by the CPP Investment Board (CPPIB) in various investments around the world. For a more detailed understanding of what the CPPIB does with your contributions visit www.cppib.com

The amount that you will receive in retirement is based on your contributions to the plan, the number of years you have contributed and the age at which you decide to begin receiving your pension.

A contributor can begin receiving the CPP retirement pension at age 60 at the earliest, and age 70 at the latest.

The plan was intended for contributors to begin receiving their pensions at age 65, but as I mentioned before, a contributor can receive it anytime between age 60 and 70. Contributors choosing to begin receiving their pension before age 65 will see a reduced pension of 0.6% per month for each month they are below the age of 65. A contributor wishing to begin their pension at age 60 instead of 65, will receive 36% less (0.6% x 60 months) than they would have at age 65.

Conversely, a contributor willing to wait after age 65 to begin receiving their retirement pension will see their pension increase 0.7% per month past the age of 65 up to a maximum of 42% more (0.7% x 60 months) at age 70. This .7% per month increase after age 65 incentivizes contributors to begin receiving their pensions later.

By registering for an account with Service Canada, you can view an online statement of your CPP contributions along with estimates of what your monthly benefit would be based on your current contributions.

In January 2021, the maximum monthly amount you could receive was $ 1,203.75 ($14,445 per year) if you chose to receive your pension at 65 at were eligible for the maximum amount. These are not large amounts and it would be virtually impossible to rely on the CPP as your sole source of income in retirement even if you have contributed the maximum amount your whole working life. With the 2019 CPP enhancements, this amount may grow to be larger portion of your retirement income.

The Quebec Pension Plan (QPP) is very similar to the CPP and also underwent and enhancement in 2019. The CPP and QPP work together in that contributions from one plan are directly transferable to the other.

The QPP is applicable to you if you have worked only in Quebec or made contributions to both the CPP and QPP, and at retirement you reside in Quebec. If you have contributed to both plans, you are considered a dual contributor and would be paid by the CPP or QPP depending on where you reside when you apply for the pension. More information on the QPP can be found at www.rrq.gouv.qc.ca

SUMMARY

Now that you have an idea of what government pensions are available, you can see that it is not a lot of money.

For example, in January 2021, if someone has made the maximum contributions their whole working lives in Canada to the CPP, they would be eligible to receive a maximum of $1,203.75 for the CPP and $615.37 for the OAS at age 65 for a grand total of $1,819.12 per month. That is a mere $21,829.44 per year which would put someone only receiving these pensions below the low income cut-off, also known as the poverty line.

The above numbers demonstrate that relying solely on government pensions in retirement is not sufficient for a comfortable retirement. Therefore it is up to the individual to save and invest for their retirement in order to supplement their government pensions with at least one other source of income.

Fortunately, the government has provided us with two types of registered savings vehicles that allow us to grow our savings without paying any income tax on dividends, capital gains or interest.

PART 3: REGISTERED INVESTMENT ACCOUNTS

Given the insufficiency of the OAS and CPP to provide for adequate income in retirement, the government has created registered savings vehicles that help Canadians invest for their retirements.

These savings vehicle are "registered" because they are not subject to investment income taxes. Investment income earned outside of registered accounts is subject to the taxation discussed in Part 1.

The first such savings vehicle, the Registered Retirement Savings Plan (RRSP), was created in 1957 as a way for Canadian employees to grow their personal retirement savings in a tax sheltered account.

A second registered savings vehicle, the Tax-Free Savings Account (TFSA), was created in 2009 as a way for all Canadians to grow their savings in a completely tax-free account for both short and long-term savings goals.

REGISTERED RETIREMENT SAVINGS PLAN (RRSP) AND REGISTERED RETIREMENT INCOME FUND (RRIF)

RRSPs were first introduced in 1957 to encourage Canadian employees to save for retirement. We often hear of people 'buying' an RRSP, but an RRSP is not something you buy, it is a type of account that investments are held in. You may hold various investments in an RRSP account including: Guaranteed Investment Certificates (GICs), bonds, stocks, mutual funds, and more. Investments in an RRSP can grow tax-free, sheltered from any taxes on investment income or capital gains until the money is withdrawn.

Contributions to an RRSP are tax deductible, meaning that whatever amount you put into an RRSP, the same amount is used to reduce your reported income, usually resulting in a tax refund. The idea is that people contribute to their RRSPs during their working years when they are in a high marginal tax bracket and withdraw the money during low income years at a lower marginal rate with the added benefit of tax sheltered growth.

It is important to emphasize that RRSP contribution room can only be accumulated from employment income. You cannot accumulate RRSP contribution room from interest, dividend or capital gains income.

You may contribute up to 18% of your employment income every year into an RRSP up to a maximum of $24,930 in 2015. Unused contribution room from previous years can be carried forward into future years. For example, if you earned $30,000 of employment income in 2014, your RRSP contribution room the following year would be $5,400 ($30,000 x 18%). You would be able to contribute up to $5,400 in 2015 and any contribution room that is unused can be used in future years.

If you have a pension plan at work, the amount that you are able to contribute to your RRSP will be reduced. No more than 18%

of your total employment income can be contributed to an RRSP and a pension plan.

When it comes time for retirement and you have decided to start withdrawing the savings that you have accumulated in your RRSP, you will need to convert your RRSP into a Registered Retirement Income Fund (RRIF) by age 71. You may however convert your RRSP to a RRIF at any age.

In order to discourage contributors from making withdrawals prior to retirement, RRSPs withdrawn prior to converting them to a RRIF will be subjected to a withholding tax that is deducted at source by your financial institution. The amount of the withdrawal is added to your annual income and taxed at your marginal rate. The amount that was withheld at source is used to offset the amount of tax you may have to pay.

In addition to the tax you must pay on withdrawals, you will not be able to recontribute the amount you withdrew at a later time.

For example, if you withdraw $5,000 from your RRSP prior to converting it to a RRIF and live in Ontario, $500 will be withheld by your financial institution and you will receive $4,500. The $5,000 you withdrew will also be added to your income and you will have to pay tax on the $5,000 withdrawal at your marginal rate, less the $500 that was already deducted.

Income received from your RRIF is taxed as pension income, which is eligible for a small tax saving measure known as the Pension Income Amount (a $2,000 non-refundable tax credit) at age 65. You also have the opportunity to split your pension income with your spouse or common law partner for potential tax savings. Despite now being classified as pension income, RRIF income is still taxed at your marginal tax rate.

RRIFs are similar to RRSPs in that your investments can still grow in a tax sheltered account, but differ in that you cannot contribute to your RRIF. When you convert your RRSPs to a RRIF you must withdraw a certain minimum percentage depending on your age.

More information on the minimum amounts that must be withdrawn from a RRIF can be found on the websites of most financial institutions.

RRSPs can also be used as a savings tool for buying your first home through the Home Buyer's Plan or to finance post-secondary education through the Lifelong Learning Plan. Withdrawals from your RRSP for these purposes are not subject to a withholding tax.

More information can be found on the Homebuyer's Plan and on the Life Long Learning Plan at the Service Canada website.

One of the main attractions to RRSPs is that contributions reduce income tax in the year they are contributed or the first 60 days of the following year. For example, if you make a $5,000 RRSP contribution in 2020, it will be as if you made $5,000 less that year in income, potentially resulting in a tax refund at both the federal and provincial levels.

More specifically, when you file your taxes for the 2020 tax year on earnings of $30,000, your $5,000 RRSP contribution is treated by the Canada Revenue Agency as if you earned $5,000 less by claiming it as a deduction from your income. You will get a refund at the 15% federal level ($750) and 5.05% at the provincial level ($252.50) for a total refund of $1,002.50 ($750 + $252.50).

If your total income had been higher, say $70,000, then your tax refund would be even larger because you would deduct the income from a higher marginal tax bracket. For example, with an income of $50,000, your marginal tax rate is 20.5% at the federal level ($1,025) and 9.15% at the provincial level ($457.50) resulting in a potential total refund of $1,482.50 ($1,025 + $457.50).

An added benefit to RRSPs is that any investment gains are tax sheltered so any capital gains, dividends or interest received in the account are not subject to tax.

It is important to note that RRSP contributions can be used to reduce your taxable income in future years when you are in a higher marginal tax bracket.

For example, using the above two scenarios of earning either $30,000 or $70,000, you can use all, some or none of your $5,000 RRSP contribution in the year you contributed to reduce your taxes. Recall, if you make a $5,000 RRSP contribution when you earned $30,000 you will get a refund of $1,002.50. But for that same $5,000 contribution, if you were earning $70,000 then you would receive a refund of $1,482.50. So if you made a $5,000 RRSP contribution when you were earning $30,000, and choose not to use the deduction in that year instead waiting until a future year when you are in a higher marginal bracket you will receive a larger refund. Unused RRSP deductions can be carried forward indefinitely.

RRSP Withdrawals – A Cautionary Tale

Based on everything you know about RRSPs up to this point, you may be surprised to know that RRSPs have been hotly debated for a long time. There is no simple answer regarding the net benefit of RRSPs. What I can tell you with certainty is that RRSPs may not beneficial to everyone and it depends on your individual circumstances.

For example, let's assume that you are approaching retirement (age 50). Imagine you receive a $40,000 inheritance and you do not know what to do with the money. Your friends, family, and financial advisor tell you to contribute to an RRSP; after all, that is what smart people do with their money.

Yes, you will get a nice tax refund. Yes, you can take that vacation you have been dreaming about for years without touching the inheritance. And yes, the inheritance itself would grow tax-free for years to come. You can understand why putting it all into an RRSP sounds like great advice. It is certainly the conventional wisdom out there. But, before coming to any conclusions, let's explore two scenarios. One in which you make the RRSP contribution and one in which you do not make the contribution.

For simplicity, let's assume it is the year 2004, you have no other income, you live in Ontario and have sufficient contribution room in your RRSP.

Scenario 1: You Make the RRSP Contribution

You make a $40,000 RRSP contribution and when you file your taxes, you receive a tax refund of $8,020 and you spend it on a Hawaiian vacation.

Your investment grows tax-free for 15 years in a conservative 5% dividend paying fund and with compounding grows to $83,157.13 when you reach age 65.

Then, let's assume that due to unforeseen circumstances you are forced to withdraw the money in your RRSP in one lump sum.

When RRSPs are withdrawn, the total amount withdrawn is taxable at the applicable marginal tax rate, so you will end up paying a total of $20,546.42 in taxes for an $83,157.13 lump sum withdrawal.

Refund Federal (15%) =	$6,000.00
Refund Ontario (5.05%) =	$2,020.00
Total Refund =	**$8,020.00**
Original Investment=	$40,000.00
5% for 15 years (gain) =	$43,157.13
Total Value after 15 years =	**$83,157.13**
Federal Tax (15%) on first $44,701 =	$6,705.15
Federal Tax (20.5%) on next $38,456.13 =	$7,883.51
Ontario Tax (5.05%) on first $40,922 =	$2,066.56
Ontario Tax (9.15%) on next $40,925 =	$3,744.64
Ontario Tax (11.16%) on next $1,310.13 =	$146.21
Total Tax (Federal and Provincial)	**$20,546.42**

In addition to the taxes you must pay for this lump sum withdrawal of your RRSP, you are now 65 and it is the year 2035. You are eligible for the OAS pension, but because the withdrawal of $83,157.13 is included as income, you are now subject to the OAS recovery tax. Due to the fact that your income exceeds the threshold for the recovery tax to take effect ($72,809), you must pay the recovery tax which is 15% of the income that exceeds the threshold:

Above Threshold: $83,157.13 - $77,580 =	$5,577.13
Recovery Tax: $5,577.13 x 15% =	$836.57

The repayment amount ($836.57), is then divided monthly and deducted from your OAS pension payments as a recovery tax, so your monthly benefit would be reduced by $69.71 ($836.57÷ 12).

Scenario 2: Invest in a Non-RRSP Account

You make a $40,000 investment in a non-RRSP account and you receive no refund. Your money grows at the same compounded annual return of 5% and you will have amassed the same $83,157.13 at age 65 in a taxable account. Recall, taxes on capital gains are only paid when you sell an investment. When you need to sell your investments, you will only have to pay $4,326.51 in taxes compared to the $20,546.42 you had to pay for withdrawing out of an RRSP. How is this possible?

To demonstrate how this is possible, when you sell your investment you will trigger a capital gain. As much as people fear incurring a capital gain, as we saw in the taxation section, capital gains are taxed at a much lower rate than other income.

For example, because your investment grew by $43,157.13 in both your taxable account and your tax sheltered RRSP account, the only difference is how the withdrawals are taxed (I have also assumed that your dividends did not result in any taxes owed). In your taxable account, you have to pay a capital gain and since only half of the gain is taxable, you must pay 15% federal tax on $21,578.57 ($3,236.79) and 5.05% provincial tax ($1,089.72) for a total of $4,326.51. As an added benefit, you will not be subject to the OAS recovery tax and receive your full OAS pension. In your tax sheltered RRSP account, you do not have to pay any capital gains tax, but the full amount of your withdrawal is taxed at your marginal rate. See below for a detailed breakdown.

Original Investment=	$40,000.00
5% for 15 years (gain) =	$43,157.13
Total Value after 15 years =	**$83,157.13**
Taxable Capital Gain (1/2 of gain) =	*$21,578.57*
Federal Tax (15%) on first $21,578.57 =	$3,236.79
Ontario Tax (5.05%) on first $21,578.57 =	$1,089.72
Total Tax (Federal and Provincial)	**$4,326.51**

While the above example is an oversimplification that excludes other tax credits, hopefully it demonstrates the potential pitfalls of RRSPs when withdrawing large amounts all at once. Please consult a qualified tax professional to determine what the actual tax consequences would be in your own personal circumstances.

WHEN AN RRSP MAKES SENSE

RRSP contributions seem to make the most sense when contributions are made when in a higher marginal tax bracket and withdrawals are made when in a lower marginal tax bracket. Let's examine two scenarios to demonstrate this.

Scenario 1: Same Tax Bracket in Retirement

Let's assume you make $40,000 a year for your entire working life of 35 years and you remain in the lowest federal and provincial tax brackets. You contribute 10% of your income to an RRSP and invest it in a fund that produces 5% annual returns that are compounded for 35 years. You then convert the RRSP to a RRIF and deplete it over the next 25 years.

Because you make an RRSP contribution, you receive a refund from the federal and provincial governments at your marginal rate:

Federal Refund= $4,000 x 15% =	$600.00
Provincial Refund = $4,000 x 5.05% =	$202.00
Total Refund =	**$802.00**

If you decide to spend the refund and do not reinvest it, in 35 years you will have amassed approximately $400,000 in your RRSP. If you decide to reinvest the refund ($802) back into your RRSP, you will have amassed approximately $477,500.

When you convert your RRSP to a RRIF and deplete it over 25 years, you will receive the following yearly income:

$400,000 ÷ 25 = $16,000 (40% of pre-retirement income)

$477,500 ÷ 25 = $19,100 (47% of pre-retirement income)

In both these circumstances, you would pay income tax at the lowest marginal rates because your income still falls within the first tax bracket for both the federal and provincial governments.

Scenario 2: Lower Tax Bracket in Retirement

Let's assume you make $60,000 a year for your entire working life of 35 years and contribute to an RRSP while in a higher marginal tax bracket than when you withdraw it. You contribute 10% of your income to an RRSP and invest it in a fund that produces 5% annual returns that are compounded for 35 years. You then convert the RRSP to a RRIF and deplete it over the next 25 years.

Because you made an RRSP contribution, you receive a refund from the federal and provincial governments at your marginal rate:

Federal Refund = $6,000 x 20.5% =	$1,230.00
Provincial Refund = $6,000 x 9.15% =	$549.00
Total Refund =	**$1,779.00**

If you decide to spend the refund ($1,779) and do not reinvest it, in 35 years you will have amassed approximately $575,000 in your RRSP. If you decide to reinvest your refund back into your RRSP along with you regular annual contributions, you will have amassed approximately $780,500.

$575,000 ÷ 25 = $23,000 (38% of pre-retirement income)

$780,500 ÷ 25 = $31,200 (52% of pre-retirement income)

In both these circumstances, you would pay income tax at the lowest marginal rates because your income falls within the first tax bracket for both the federal and provincial governments. This presents an advantage to you because you contributed at a higher marginal tax rate and are withdrawing at a lower marginal tax rate.

In both scenarios, if you do not invest your refund back into your RRSP, you will be able to replace approximately 40% of your pre-retirement income.

It is interesting to note that in the scenario in which you were in a higher marginal tax rate and reinvested your refund, you were able to generate a superior return and replace 52% of your pre-retirement income as opposed to 47% when you were in a lower tax bracket. This is due to reinvesting a larger amount and the power of compounding.

Based on the above scenarios, RRSPs seem to have their biggest benefit for high income individuals who can receive a tax refund at a high marginal tax rate and then withdraw their money at a much lower rate and reinvest their tax refund back into their RRSP or other investments.

Are RRSPs a Good Choice For Younger Canadians?

There are several challenges regarding RRSPs:

- You may not currently be in a high tax bracket;

- You have to guess what tax rates will be 30 to 40 years from now;

- Should you need to withdraw your RRSP for an emergency, you will have to pay a large portion in taxes;

- You may be tempted to spend your refund;

- Income received from RRSPs may affect eligibility for OAS and other benefits.

Unfortunately there is no easy answer as to whether or not RRSPs are right for you because the answer is highly dependent on your personal circumstances and what the future will be 30-40 years from now. The original intention of RRSPs was for Canadian workers to contribute during high income years, grow their savings tax-free, and then to gradually withdraw contributions during lower income years, but this may not be the case for everyone.

One sure-fire way millennials can take advantage of RRSPs are by using them as a savings vehicle for a down payment on their first homes through the Home Buyer's Plan mentioned earlier. You can withdraw up to $35,000 out of your RRSP to use as a down payment on your first home without paying any taxes on the withdrawals. The withdrawn money then has to be paid back into the RRSP interest-free over a maximum time span of 15 years beginning the year following the year the withdrawal is made.

I urge you to further educate yourself on this topic and determine if making RRSP contributions is right for you and to explore alternative savings vehicles such as Tax-Free Savings Accounts (TFSAs) that offer more flexibility.

TAX-FREE SAVINGS ACCOUNT (TFSA)

Since 2009, eligible Canadian residents aged 18 or older are able to make a registered contribution to a Tax-Free Savings Account (TFSA) . In 2009, the initial annual contribution limit was $5,000 and has since grown to $6,000 in 2021.

Unlike RRSPs, TFSA contribution room is not dependent on employment income, or any other income. Every legal Canadian resident can accumulate TFSA contribution room regardless of their employment status or income.

Unused contribution room can be carried over to future years, but only for the years that you were over the age of 18. For example, if you have never made a TFSA contribution and you were over the age of 18 in 2009, by 2021 you could contribute $75,500.00

It is important to note that any contributions that exceed the maximum amount are heavily taxed and can result in a large amount of tax owing. So do not over contribute to a TFSA.

Withdrawals from a TFSA can be re-contributed in subsequent years including any gains. For example, if you began contributing to your TFSA in 2009 and made the maximum contributions every year until 2021 you would have contributed $75,500.00. If you decide to withdraw your entire TFSA contributions, you will have to wait until January 1 of the following year to re-contribute. As of the following January 1st, you can re-contribute the entire amount you withdrew along with the new annual contribution amount you are entitled to for that year.

For example, let's assume your contributions from 2009-2021 had grown to $100,000.00 as a result of investment gains, and you decide to withdraw the full $100,000.00. The following year you would be able to re-contribute the entire $100,000.00 plus the annual amount you are entitled to for that year.

The two main benefits of TFSAs are that investment income earned in the account and withdrawals are tax-free so any interest, dividends or capital gains earned in the account are not taxed. The account holder can withdraw money from the account at any time, without having to pay any tax on the withdrawals.

The name Tax-Free Savings Account is somewhat of a misnomer because it is not limited to conventional savings accounts. TFSAs can hold investments such as bonds, stocks, mutual funds, Exchange Traded Funds (ETFs), Guaranteed Investment Certificates (GICs) and income trusts.

RRSP VS TFSA

To demonstrate how RRSPs differ from TFSAs, let's compare three scenarios in which you earn $10,000 of employment income and would like to invest it for retirement. You are unsure if you should invest the money in an RRSP or TFSA. In the first scenario, you expect to be in the same tax bracket in retirement as you are now. In the second scenario, you expect to be in a lower tax bracket in retirement. In the third scenario, you expect to be in higher tax bracket in retirement.

Let's assume that you invest the $10,000 in a fund that produces a 5% annual compounded growth rate over 25 years:

Scenario 1: Same Tax Bracket in Retirement

Let's assume your combined (federal and provincial) marginal tax rate is 35% and remains the same when you withdraw the total amount.

Because you earned the $10,000 of employment income, you will have to pay tax on your earnings at a marginal rate of 35% and pay $3,500 in tax. If you choose to contribute to an RRSP, you will receive the $3,500 back as a refund when you file your taxes so the total tax paid on $10,000 is zero. Conversely, for the same $10,000 of employment income, if you chose to contribute to a TFSA you will not get a tax refund and will only have $6,500 to invest.

Table 6 - RRSP vs. TFSA: Same Tax Bracket in Retirement

	RRSP	TFSA
Income Before Tax	$10,000.00	$10,000.00
Tax Paid (35%)	$0.00	$3,500.00
Amount Invested	$10,000.00	$6,500.00
Total Value After 25 Years	$33,863.55	$22,011.31
Tax for Withdrawing Total Amount (35%)	$11,852.24	$0.00
Net Amount Received	$22,011.31	$22,011.31

As you can see, in a scenario in which you will be in the same marginal tax bracket in retirement, there is no difference between choosing an RRSP or TFSA.

Scenario 2: Lower Tax Bracket in Retirement

Now let's assume your combined marginal tax rate is 35% when you contribute to your RRSP and 20% when you withdraw the total amount in retirement.

Table 7 - RRSP vs. TFSA: Lower Tax Bracket in Retirement

	RRSP	TFSA
Income Before Tax	$10,000.00	$10,000.00
Tax Paid (35%)	$0.00	$3,500.00
Amount Invested	$10,000.00	$6,500.00
Total Value After 25 Years	$33,863.55	$22,011.31
Tax for Withdrawing Total Amount (20%)	$6,772.71	$0.00
Net Amount Received	$27,090.84	$22,011.31

In a scenario in which you are in a lower tax bracket in retirement, the $10,000 contributed to your RRSP is a clear winner.

Scenario 3: Higher Tax Bracket in Retirement

Finally, let's flip the second scenario around and assume that your combined marginal tax rate is 20% when you contribute to your RRSP and 35% when you withdraw the total amount in retirement.

Table 8 - RRSP vs. TFSA: Higher Tax Bracket in Retirement

	RRSP	TFSA
Income Before Tax	$10,000.00	$10,000.00
Tax Paid (20%)	$0.00	$2,000.00
Amount Invested	$10,000.00	$8,000.00
Total Value After 25 Years	$33,863.55	$27,090.84
Tax for Withdrawing Total Amount (35%)	$11,852.24	$0.00
Net Amount Received	$22,011.31	$27,090.84

As you might have expected, in a scenario in which you are in a higher tax bracket in retirement, the $10,000 contributed to your TFSA is a clear winner.

THE CHOICE IS YOURS

Younger generations have more choice when it comes to saving for their retirements than their parent's generation. With the introduction of the TFSA in 2009, there are now two types of registered savings vehicles that allow Canadians to grow their savings in a tax sheltered account.

However, having two options can sometimes lead to confusion on which savings vehicle is best.

There is no easy answer to this question as it depends on many factors. On the one hand, TFSAs offer flexibility to meet your short and long-term savings goals. On the other hand, RRSPs offer an immediate tax deduction to save for longer term goals such as a down payment for your first home, post-secondary education or your retirement.

Regardless of what type of account you choose to save for retirement, your investment mix will determine your overall returns.

The following section will examine what investment options are available to you: savings accounts, Guaranteed Investment Certificates (GICs), stocks, mutual funds, Exchange Traded Funds (ETFs) and income trusts.

PART 4: INVESTMENT OPTIONS

There are numerous types of investment options out there, however considering the scope of this book, there are generally three types of investments that are available to the millennial investor: savings accounts, Guaranteed Investment Certificates (GICs) and equity investments.

Savings Accounts

Why Do People Invest in Savings Accounts?

People invest in savings accounts for the safety, flexibility, convenience, understandability, and comparatively higher interest rate than a chequing account.

In the unlikely case of a bank failure, most deposits in savings accounts are insured by the Canada Deposit and Insurance Corporation (CDIC) up to $100,000. For further information, I strongly encourage you to visit the CDIC website to see what deposits are insured and what is not. You can access the CDIC's website at www.cdic.ca.

How Do Savings Accounts Work?

Most people are familiar with and likely even have a savings account. As of January 2021, most of the major banks in Canada (Bank of Montreal, TD, CIBC, Royal Bank, Scotia Bank) pay next to nothing in interest on your deposits.

With the advent of online (digital only) banking, many online banking institutions began offering high interest savings accounts that paid higher interest rates than conventional savings accounts offered by major banks.

The most important factor to consider when making a decision about opening a savings account is to understand the fees associated with them. Most savings accounts are free to open, but sometimes charge fees for withdrawals, transfers and even mailing you a statement. With the interest on your deposits already very low, the fees that financial institutions charge can negate any savings you have accumulated.

Guaranteed Investment Certificates (GICs)

Guaranteed Investment Certificates (GICs) are investment products that are offered by financial institutions that pay a guaranteed rate of return on the money you invest over a fixed amount of time.

Nearly all GICs operate on the notion of earning interest on principal. The *principal* is your initial investment in a GIC. *Interest* is the income you expect to receive from the borrower of your principal before they pay the principal back. The *interest rate* is the percentage of interest that must be paid to you by the borrower on an annual basis.

For example, if you invest $10,000 (principal) in a GIC that pays you 2% annually (interest rate) you will earn $20 (interest) at the end of one year.

An important term in the world of investing is *yield*. The yield on an investment is the percentage of your principal that you receive as income on an annual basis. The previous example of a

$10,000 GIC investment earning 2% interest would have a yield of 2% ($20) because that is the percentage of your principal that you receive as income.

Why Do People Invest in GICs?

Investors generally prefer GICs over savings accounts because of the higher interest rates they offer along with the same CDIC insurance and risk protection. GICs offer higher interest yields than savings accounts because withdrawals are not as flexible (more on this below). GICs are usually used by investors who are not comfortable with any risk for short to medium term savings goals in which they do not want to put their investment principal at risk.

GICs are guaranteed and considered one of the safest investments because when you invest in a GIC they are insured by the CDIC. The CDIC insures GICs with an original term of five years or less and up to $100,000 if the institution you are purchasing the GIC from is a member.

How Do GICs Work?

The amount you invest, your principal, will earn interest at pre-determined rate for a fixed amount of time. The amount of time that you must leave your money in a GIC varies from one month to 10 years and is known as a *term*. Once the term has passed, your investment has reached *maturity*. Once your investment has 'matured', you get your principal back along with any interest that is owed. GICs also differ in when you are allowed to withdraw your investment (principal and interest), the interest paid on the principal, the frequency of interest payments and whether the interest paid can be compounded. Here is a very simple example:

If you invest $1,000 on January 1 in a GIC for a term of one year at an annual interest rate of 2%, the following January 1, your GIC will have 'matured' and your investment will now be worth $1,020. The $1,020 is comprised of the principal you invested

($1,000) and the interest you earned on that principal $20 ($1,000 x 2%) over the course of the year.

What to Consider When Choosing a GIC?

When comparing GICs, the key components to examine are:

- **Term Length** – The amount of time that you must leave your money invested in the GIC in order to reach full maturity. The length of the term that you choose is based on your investment goals. For example, if you are saving up for a down payment on a home and expect to need the money in two years, a GIC with a term of two years may be a logical choice.

- **Payment Frequency** – The length of time an investor must wait to receive an interest payment. For example: monthly, quarterly (every 3 months), semi-annually (every 6 months), annually, or at maturity (end of the term). Most GICs offer an annual payment frequency for interest.

- **Redeemability** – The option to redeem your investment (principal and earned interest) before maturity without incurring penalties.

- **Minimum Investment** – The minimum amount of money you must invest in the GIC, usually $500.

- **Compoundable** – Allows interest earned during the term be reinvested and added to the principal.

- **Compound Frequency** – How often the interest is reinvested back into the principal for the duration of the term.

- **Interest Rate (Yield)** – The rate of interest the GIC pays on the principal.

Now let's compare two GICs:

	GIC 1	GIC 2
Term (years)	5	5
Payment Frequency	Annual	Annual
Redeemable	No	No

Compoundable	No	Yes
Compound Frequency	Annual	Annual
Interest Rate	2%	2%
Amount Invested	$10,000.00	$10,000.00

Here are the values after five years for each GIC:

Year	GIC 1		GIC 2	
	Principal	Interest	Principal	Interest
1	$10,000.00	$200.00	$10,000.00	$200.00
2	$10,000.00	$200.00	$10,200.00	$204.00
3	$10,000.00	$200.00	$10,404.00	$208.08
4	$10,000.00	$200.00	$10,612.08	$212.24
5	$10,000.00	$200.00	$10,824.32	$216.49
	Total Interest	$1,000.00	Total Interest	$1,040.81
	Value after 5 years	$11,000.00	Value after 5 years	$11,040.81

As you can see from the above example; by everything else remaining equal except for the ability to compound, you are able to generate a superior return at the end of the term. With the option to compound the interest earned at the end of every year, $10,000 invested at a 2% interest rate with compounding matured into $11,040.81 vs. $11,000 at the end of the fifth year.

$40.81 may not seem like much, especially over five years, but over longer periods of time and higher rates of interest, compounding can lead to extraordinary returns as we will see later.

Market-Linked GICs

A newer form of GIC is a market-linked GIC. These GICs still offer 100% guaranteed principal protection along with the potential for a higher rate of return if whatever investment the GIC is linked to appreciates, up to a maximum. Market-linked GICs can be linked to U.S., Canadian and Global stock markets. A market-linked GIC can also be linked to specific market sectors or a portfolio of investments chosen by the issuer.

In other words, your principal is still guaranteed to be there when you need it and in exchange for a smaller guaranteed return, you have the possibility to get a higher return if the investment the GIC is linked to does better than the minimum return. Let's look at an example from RBC:

- Term to Maturity: 5 years
- Linked to S&P 500 (U.S. Stock Market Index)
- Minimum Total Return (%): 5.25%
- Maximum Total Return (%): 21.00%

Let's assume you have $10,000 to invest and will not need the money for five years. Based on the above information, if you leave your principal in the market-linked GIC for five years you will receive a minimum return of 5.25%. But, depending on the performance of the U.S. stock market, you may receive up to a maximum return of 21% for the term of five years. We will examine three scenarios in which the market index is up 20%, down 20% and up 35%.

Scenario 1: Market Index is Up 20%

If the underlying index increases 20% over the five year term of the GIC, this would indicate an increase of 20% in the index. In this scenario, the increase is above the minimum of 5.25% and below the maximum of 21% so you would receive 100% of your principal plus a 20% return on your investment.

Total investment value: $12,000. You will get your $10,000 back plus the 20% you earned because the index went up by 20% during that time which is $2,000 ($10,000 x 20%).

Scenario 2: Market Index is Down 20%

If the underlying index decreases by 20% over the five year term of the GIC, you would receive 100% of your principal plus the 5.25% guaranteed minimum return set out at the time of purchase.

Total investment value: $10,525. You will get your $10,000 back plus the 5.25% minimum return which is $525 ($10,000 x 5.25%).

Scenario 3: Market Index is Up 35%

If the underlying index increases by 35% over the five year term of the GIC, this would indicate an increase of 35% in the index. In this scenario, since the increase is above the maximum, you would receive 100% of your principal plus the 21% maximum return set out at the time of purchase.

Total investment value: $12,100. You will get your $10,000 back plus the 21% you earned because you have reached the maximum return. Even though the market was up by 35%, your maximum gain is limited to $2,100 ($10,000 x 21%).

Market-linked GICs are particularly interesting as they may provide an investor who does not want any risk some chance for a higher return. On the surface, they seem like the best of both worlds, 100% principal protection with the potential to participate in market gains without the risk. Essentially the tradeoff is the GIC issuer will pay you a lower guaranteed return, and limit your maximum gain.

However, if the market doesn't go the way you hope, you will make less than you would have if you had put your investment in a traditional GIC. For example, since the minimum return for this GIC is 5.25% for five years, it amounts to a 1.05% annual return compared to a classic GIC annual return of 2%. Of note, even though the gain you receive on your investment is from the market-linked GIC increasing in value, the gain is still taxed as interest income.

GIC Summary

GICs can provide investors who are not comfortable with risk a convenient and low cost way to save. GICs do not carry practically any risk, but they also do not offer much in the way of return. GICs generally pay a higher interest rate yield than savings accounts, however, still do not offer a yield that is sufficient to keep pace with inflation. A helpful GIC resource is CANNEX: http://www.cannex.com

What Are The Risks Associated With Savings Accounts and GIC?

The main risk factor associated with savings accounts and GICs is not losing your investment as both types of investments are protected by the CDIC, but rather from *inflation risk.*

Inflation Risk

Inflation is the tendency of the prices of goods and services to increase over time. So as inflation rises, one dollar buys fewer goods and services in the future.

Put another way, the value of a dollar decreases over time because inflation reduces purchasing power. Purchasing power is the real value of money and when inflation rises the purchasing power of one dollar decreases.

For example, if the inflation rate is 3% per year then a good or service that cost $100 today will cost $103 a year later, thus reducing the purchasing power of $100. In other words, the $100 is no longer sufficient to purchase the same good or service it did a year ago.

How Is Inflation Measured?

Canada's central bank, the Bank of Canada, is responsible for preserving the value of money by keeping inflation low and stable. The Bank of Canada is a crown corporation that is owned by the Government of Canada, but is separate from the political process. The most popular way that inflation is measured is called the Consumer Price Index (CPI). The Bank of Canada uses the CPI in an attempt to track the changes in consumer prices by using a theoretical basket of goods and services to compare the change in consumer prices over time.

For example, when you hear in the news that "Canada's annual inflation was 2.4%", it means that the theoretical basket of goods and services that the Bank of Canada uses to measure inflation increased by 2.4% and the same basket is 2.4% more expensive than it was the same time a year ago. It does not necessarily mean that your personal purchasing power has decreased by 2.4%, but that the prices of goods and services in the Bank of Canada's theoretical basket increased by 2.4%.

For example, if the Bank of Canada released its CPI data indicating that inflation had risen 2.4% from the same time the previous year. If you were to read beyond the headline, it may be that most of the increase in the CPI was due to an increase in the price of natural gas, cigarettes and bacon. Now, if you do not smoke, heat and cool your home with natural gas or eat bacon every morning, your purchasing power may not have decreased by 2.4%.

The CPI is also a national measure and may not accurately reflect the level of consumer prices in the area of the country in which you live, although provincial CPI data is also available at the Bank of Canada's website at www.bankofcanada.ca

The CPI attracts the most headlines and discussion, but it is also the most volatile. The more stable and some would say more important measure of inflation is the Core Consumer Price Index (Core CPI). This measure removes eight of the most volatile components of the CPI such as fruits, vegetables, gasoline, fuel oil, natural gas, mortgage interest, intercity transportation, and tobacco products in an attempt to get a better sense of the real underlying trend of inflation.

The Bank of Canada monitors inflation very carefully. In fact, one of the primary reasons for a central bank's existence is to monitor inflation and maintain inflation between 1-3% per year. The Bank of Canada uses what is known as monetary policy to attempt to maintain inflation between its 1-3% target range to encourage price stability.

One of the tools the Bank of Canada can use is setting the Bank of Canada's key interest rate. At the time of writing this book, the rate is 0.50%. Without going into too much detail and macroeconomic theory, this rate heavily influences other rates such as consumer loans, mortgages and virtually all other interest rates in Canada.

The Bank of Canada can use monetary policy to control the level of inflation by raising or lowering its key interest rate. For example, if the Bank of Canada believes that inflation will exceed its target range of 1-3%, it can adjust its key interest rate by increasing or decreasing it to a level that will encourage price stability and maintain purchasing power.

What Causes Inflation?

Economics uses mostly quantitative analysis, but it is an art and not a science. Economics relies on theories that are still being hotly debated today and there is no one single correct answer for what causes inflation. Two prevailing theories are the "demand pull" theory and "cost push" theory.

The demand pull inflation theory uses the law of supply and demand to explain inflation. Essentially, it is the idea that if demand exceeds supply, the price of a good will increase so the demand is 'pulling' prices higher.

The cost push theory explains inflation as when a company's costs increase they must increase the price of their goods to maintain their profits so the cost of a supplier's good is 'pushing' prices higher.

Of course there are other theories and the correct answer of what causes inflation is undoubtedly a combination of all existing theories.

The Bank of Canada has an inflation calculator on its website that has historical data going back 100 years. It allows you to see what any amount of money in 'current' dollars would be required to purchase the same basket of goods and services in the past. For example, the same basket of goods and services purchased for $100 in 2002 would cost $124.41 in 2014.

Back to Inflation Risk

Inflation risk is the risk that inflation rates will change significantly from the time that a bond investor purchased a bond to the maturity date.

Let's use an example of you buying a GIC for $10,000 that pays you 4% annually for five years. Let's also assume that when you bought the GIC, you expected inflation to remain consistent at 2% per year for the duration of the bond, resulting in a 'real' (inflation-adjusted) interest rate of 2% (4% interest payment − 2% inflation).

To demonstrate inflation risk, let's use two scenarios. The first scenario will demonstrate inflation working against your favour and the second will demonstrate inflation working in your favour.

In the first scenario of an increasing inflation environment, let's assume that inflation slowly increases at a rate of 0.25% per year beyond your 2% inflation assumption for the duration of the bond.

Scenario 1

Year	Interest Payment	Inflation (%)	Inflation ($)	"Real" Return
1	$400	2.00	$200	$200
2	$400	2.25	$225	$175
3	$400	2.50	$250	$150
4	$400	2.75	$275	$125
5	$400	3.00	$300	$100
Total	$2,000		$1,250	$750

After five years, you will receive your $10,000 back and you will have collected $2,000 in interest payments over the five years. How much have you really made though after inflation? The answer is only $750 due to effects of increasing inflation reducing the real value of the fixed interest payments each year.

Conversely, with risk there is also reward. In the second scenario of a decreasing inflation environment, let's assume that inflation slowly decreases at rate of 0.25% per year below the 2% inflation assumption for the duration of the bond.

Scenario 2

Year	Interest Payment	Inflation (%)	Inflation ($)	"Real" Return
1	$400	2.00	$200	$200
2	$400	1.75	$175	$225
3	$400	1.50	$150	$250
4	$400	1.25	$125	$275
5	$400	1.00	$100	$300
Total	$2,000		$750	$1,250

In this scenario, you will receive your $10,000 back and you will have collected the same $2,000 in interest payments over five years, but your real inflation-adjusted return is $1,250.

Summary of Savings Accounts and GICs

Fixed income investments such as savings accounts and GICs, offer younger Canadians a convenient and low cost way to start saving for their retirements. However, in the current low interest rate environment, it will be next to impossible to find the kind of investment returns necessary to fund your retirement using only savings accounts and GICs.

High interest rates were common in our parent's generation. They could routinely earn double-digit interest rates from GICs, savings bonds and even regular savings accounts. Although these high interest rates may seem impressive, they occurred during relatively high inflation years and did more to preserve wealth than build it.

Savings accounts and GICs certainly have a place in most people's portfolios, but younger investors may want to add equity investments as a significant portion of their investment portfolios to truly accumulate wealth.

EQUITY INVESTMENTS

Stocks

Stocks are pieces of ownership in a corporation that investors buy and sell on *stock exchanges*. The process of buying or selling a stock is called a "trade". Investors trade money for stocks and stocks for money. Stocks trade on stock exchanges around the world and can be bought and sold by institutions and members of the public.

Corporations can either be privately owned and do not trade on stock exchanges or can be publicly owned. Publicly owned means that shares of the corporation trade on a stock exchange and can be bought and sold by members of the general public. Most corporations begin as private, but when future growth requires financing, they 'go public' and offer shares of the business for sale to investors in exchange for their money.

The main stock exchange in Canada is the Toronto Stock Exchange (TSX). In the U.S., the two major stock exchanges are the New York Stock Exchange (NYSE) and the NASDAQ stock exchange. Stocks are also known as shares, equity or common stock and represent a claim on a corporation's earnings and assets.

Stock = Share = Equity = Common Stock

Some corporations pay a portion of their earnings directly to shareholders on a regular basis in the form of a dividend. These corporations have policies in place that guide the management's decision on the percentage of earnings that will be paid to shareholders in the form of a dividend.

Shareholders can have voting rights and can vote who will run the company, however there is no requirement to vote. Shareholders place their trust in the board of directors and management to make decisions on their behalf.

Why Do People Invest in Stocks?

Some investors primarily buy shares of a corporation with the expectation that the price of the shares will increase so that they can sell their shares at a higher price for a capital gain. Other investors primarily buy stocks to receive a stream of income from the corporation's dividend. Some investors even do both!

No other type of investment has created as much wealth as stocks. Looking at data going back over 100 years, in the long run the average annual return of stocks is about 10-12%. Remember that a return of 10-12% does not mean that stocks move up 10-12% every year. This return is a long-term average with some years seeing declines of over 30%, other years seeing gains of over 30% and everything in between.

How Are Stocks Bought and Sold?

Before getting into particulars of individual stocks, let's first discuss how individual stocks are bought and sold. In order to buy or sell a stock you must use a stock broker who places your order to a stock exchange. This is called placing a 'trade'.

There are two types of brokers: discount brokers and full service brokers. Discount brokers are only there to place trades on your behalf, while full service brokers may also provide advice and recommendations as well as placing your order to the exchange.

Both discount and full service brokers charge commissions to buy and sell shares in the stock market, with the commissions charged by full service brokers far exceeding those charged by discount brokers. Virtually all Canadian banks offer both discount and full service brokers.

Stock Market Indexes

There are over 100,000 corporations that trade on stock exchanges around the world. Most industrialized countries have indexes that include a basket of stocks that trade in that country. Many indexes are meant to provide a snapshot of the performance of a wide breadth of stocks that trade in that country.

In Canada, the main index that is quoted in the evening news is the TSX Composite Index. In the United States, the three major stock market indexes are the Dow Jones Industrial Average, the Standard and Poor's (S&P) 500 Index and the NASDAQ Composite Index.

The TSX Composite Index

The TSX Composite Index includes approximately 250 of Canada's largest publicly traded corporations. The number of corporations can either increase or decrease depending on whether or not a corporation meets the inclusion criteria.

Inclusion in the index is based on a set of criteria with the most important being market capitalization. *Market capitalization* or "market cap" for short, is the total market value of a company's stock currently held by all its shareholders. Market cap is calculated by multiplying the price of a share by the number of common shares outstanding.

So in essence, the bigger the corporation's market cap is, the more of a weighting it will get in the overall index.

For example, at the time of writing, the largest public corporation in Canada in terms of market cap is the Royal Bank of Canada (RBC) at approximately 110 billion dollars. As a result, it has the largest weighting in the TSX Composite Index of approximately 6.25%. This means that although RBC is only one of approximately 250 corporations, it represents a disproportionately large share of the index due to its large market cap.

If the TSX Composite Index were an equal weight index, in which each corporation in the index has the same weight regardless of market cap, RBC would only have a weighting of 0.4% (1/250).

Table 10 on is a breakdown of the weighting of each sector of the TSX Composite Index as of January, 2021. The index is heavily weighted in financial corporations, accounting for around a third of the index.

Table 9 - TSX Index Sector Weighting

Sector	Weighting (%)
Financials (Banks, Insurance)	30
Energy (Oil and Gas)	11
Materials (Mining)	14
Industrials	12.5
Consumer Discretionary	4
Communication Services	5
Health Care	1
Consumer Staples	4
Information Technology	10
Utilities	5
Real Estate	5

The Dow Jones Industrial Average

The Dow Jones Industrial Average or more commonly referred to as the "Dow", is a price-weighted index that is comprised of 30 stocks that represent the diverse sectors of the U.S. economy. Corporations can be added or withdrawn from the index, but it will always be comprised of 30 corporations. It has some of the most recognizable corporations in the world such as McDonalds, Disney, Microsoft, Visa, Wal-Mart and Apple just to name a few.

As a price-weighted index, the higher the price of a stock, the more weight it receives in the index. For example, at the time of writing in January 2021, United Health Group Inc. is the component with the highest price at approximately $355 a share, so it receives a weighting of 7.4%. Compare that to Cisco Systems with a price of approximately $45 a share, which receives a weighting of approximately 1%.

The Standard and Poor's (S&P) 500 Index

The S&P 500 Index is a market cap weighted index that includes approximately 500 large U.S. corporations. It is considered the best gauge of the U.S. market since it has 500 stocks compared to only 30 in the Dow.

Like the TSX Composite Index, the larger a corporation's market cap, the larger weight it receives in the index. At the time of writing, Apple was the largest U.S. public corporation by market cap, so it accounts for the largest weighting of the S&P 500. Table 11 lists the five corporations with the largest weightings in the S&P as of January 2021.

Table 10 - Top 5 Corporations by Weighting in the S&P 500

	Corporation
1	Apple
2	Microsoft
3	Amazon.com
4	Facebook
5	Tesla

The NASDAQ Composite Index

The NASDAQ Composite Index comprises over 3000 stocks that trade on the NASDAQ stock exchange. The NASDAQ Composite Index is a market cap weighted index. Shares listed on the NASDAQ tend to be more heavily weighted in the technology and internet sectors like Facebook, Amazon, and Apple. As a result, the NASDAQ Composite Index has a disproportionately large weighting of high growth oriented stocks than stocks listed in the Dow Jones Industrial Average and S&P 500 Index.

Stock Quote

Buyers and sellers come together in the stock market and shares trade electronically from 09:30 AM to 4:00 PM Eastern Time during business days. If there a more buyers for a stock than there are sellers, the price will increase. Conversely, if there are more sellers for a stock than buyers, the price will decrease. This is the law of supply and demand you learned in your high school economics class in action. The price of a stock only represents what the last price paid for the shares were.

A stock quote is called a quote because it provides information on what investors are offering (quoting) to buy or sell shares. Below is a typical stock quote and we'll take some time to famil-iarize ourselves with the information contained within it using the Toronto-Dominion (TD) bank as an example.

$57.42
Change: -0.45 (-0.86%)

Open:	$57.15	**EPS:**	4.09
High:	$57.46	**Dividend:**	$0.47
Low:	$57.11	**Yield:**	3.31%
Prev. Close:	$57.87	**Div Frequency:**	Quarterly
Bid:	$57.42	**P/E Ratio:**	13.9
Ask:	$57.43	**Beta:**	0.725
Exchange:	TSX		

The price in bold, $57.42 is the last price paid for a share. It is also known as the Market Price.

Change: The change in price since the close of the market the previous trading day (Prev. Close). This will either be in red, rep-resenting a decline, or green representing an increase.

Open: The price of the stock at the market open. In this case, the first trade of the day was at a price of $57.15.

High: The highest price paid for the stock throughout the day. In this case, the highest price paid was $57.46.

Low: The lowest price paid for the stock throughout the day. In this case, the lowest price paid was $57.11.

Previous (Prev) Close: The price of the stock at the close of trade on the previous business day. In this case, the last trade of the previous business day was $57.87.

Bid: The price a buyer is offering to pay a seller for the stock. In this case, the buyer is proposing (bidding) to pay $57.42.

Ask: The price a seller is willing to sell their shares at. This price is usually more than or equal to the market price. In this case, the seller is proposing (asking) to sell their shares for $57.43.

Earnings per Share (EPS): The corporation's total earnings divided by the number of shares outstanding. The EPS is useful to determine if a company is profitable.

Dividend: The cash amount that is paid on a per share basis. In this case, one share entitles the shareholder to $0.47 per share owned.

Dividend (Div) Frequency: How often the dividend is paid. In this case, it is quarterly (every 3 months) so you would receive $0.47 per share for every share you own every three months, or 4 payments a year. The annual dividend would be $0.47 x 4 = $1.88 per share.

Dividend (Yield): The percentage yield on an annual basis that the dividend provides. If you were to buy 1 share of TD stock today at $57.42 you will be paid $1.88 in dividends over the next year. The yield (3.31%) is calculated by dividing the annual dividend by the price of the shares ($1.88/$57.42).

Price to Earnings (P/E) Ratio: The P/E ratio is the price of the stock divided by the Earnings per Share (EPS). The P/E ratio is useful in determining how cheap or expensive a stock is relative to similar companies.

Exchange: The exchange that the shares of the corporation trade on. In this case, shares of TD trade on the Toronto Stock Exchange (TSX).

Beta: The volatility of a stock compared the stock market as a whole. In this case, the stock has a beta of .725 which means in theory that the stock is 72.5% as volatile as the market as a whole. Therefore it is less volatile than the entire stock market. By definition, the market has a beta of 1.0 and individual stocks are ranked according to how much they deviate from the market. A stock that is more volatile than the market over time has a beta above 1.0. If a stock is less volatile than the market, the stock's beta is less than 1.0. Theoretically, high-beta (>1) stocks are more volatile and low-beta (<1) stocks are less volatile than the market as a whole.

How Do People Buy and Sell Stocks?

For the vast majority of investors, in order to buy a stock you will first need to transfer money from your bank account to an investment brokerage account.

Market and Limit Orders

When placing a buy or sell order with a broker, you will be asked what type of order you are requesting. The two main types of stock market orders are market and limit orders.

A market order is a request to buy or sell a stock at the best price the market is offering. A limit order is a request to buy or sell a stock for a certain price or better. A limit order can be set at any time, and when the 'ask' price of a stock equals your 'bid' price or vice versa, the trade will be executed.

It is advisable to always use limit orders so that you can be sure of what price you will buy or sell a stock for. It also does not require you to monitor the price of the stock throughout the day.

Ticker Symbols

All shares of publicly traded corporations trade using "ticker" symbols on stock exchanges. They are usually 1 to 4 letter symbols that often abbreviate the name of corporations. For example, Bank of Montreal's ticker symbol is BMO, while Apple's ticker symbol is AAPL. Harley Davidson motorcycles uses the ticker symbol HOG as a reference to Harley Davidson enthusiasts calling their motorcycles "Hogs".

The ticker symbol of a corporation can be found at the corporation's website in the Investor Relations section or by a simple internet search. In order to place a trade or obtain a quote, you must know the corporation's ticker symbol.

How to Buy and Sell Stocks

Below is an example of an order screen for entering an order to place a trade (buy or sell a stock). All brokerage sites will have a slightly different interface, but all will have the following main components: Account, Action, Quantity, Symbol, Market, and Price.

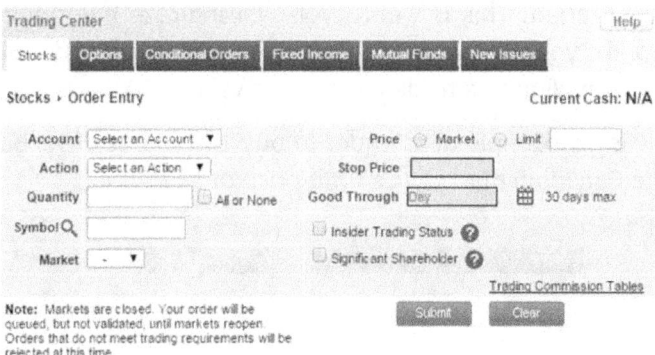

Account: This is where you will select which stock trading account you wish to buy a stock for or sell a stock from if you have more than one.

Action: This is where you will select which action you would like to take, buy or sell.

Quantity: This is where you will select how many shares you would like to buy or sell. The 'all or none' option indicates whether you would like the entire trade to be placed or not at all. For example, it you place an order to buy 100 shares of TD

Bank at $52.25, the broker will not fill the order unless they can obtain all 100 shares at $52.25 or lower. All or none orders are permitted on U.S. markets only.

Symbol: This is where you would input the ticker symbol of the stock you would like to trade.

Market: This is where you would select which market the stock is listed, Canadian or U.S.

Price: This is where you would select the type or order, either market or limit. If the 'market' option is selected, you will buy or sell the stock at the best available price that is currently being offered by other market participants, which could be better or worse than you expect. If you select the 'limit' option, you specify at what price you would like to buy or sell the stock for and are guaranteed that price or better.

Good Through: This is where you will indicate how long you would like your order to remain valid if you are using a limit order. The maximum a trade can remain valid is 30 days.

Below is an example of an order to buy 100 shares of TD Bank, on the Canadian market at a limit price of $52.25.

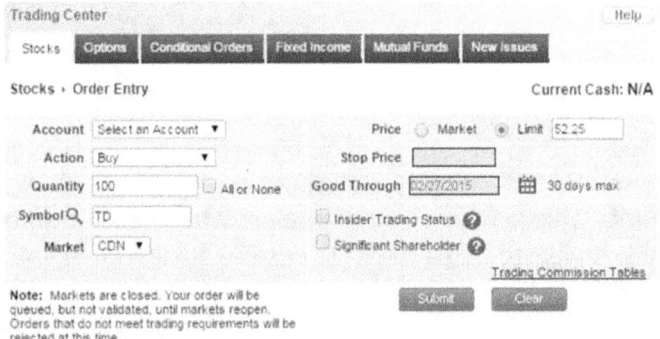

Once your order is placed, you will be taken to another screen that will ask you to confirm the order and enter a trading password.

Most discount brokers offer a complete tutorial on how to use their trading platform. At every stage of the process, there is usually a 'help' button to assist you with any terms that you are not familiar with.

What Is a Stock Worth?

The short answer is a stock is worth what someone else is willing to pay for it. The long and complicated answer is that a stock's price is determined by what the expected future earnings of the corporation will be. In other words, the price of a stock is not what the corporation is currently earning, but what investors believe the corporation will earn in the future.

For example, if you were interested in buying shares of Rogers Communications, it would be because you believe that Rogers will continue to exist into the foreseeable future and will earn money. It would not be logical to buy a stock in a company you and other investors believe will go out of business in a few years. The price of one share of Rogers's stock is a reflection of what investors believe Rogers will earn in the foreseeable future.

The whole essence of stock investing is being able to determine if the market price of a stock is an accurate reflection of the underlying value of the corporation. The price of a stock and the value of the corporation are supposed to equal, but like in any market that is subject to the law of supply and demand, this is not always the case. The entire investment industry is essentially dedicated to determining if the current market price of a stock is an accurate reflection of the stock's underlying value.

To put it simply, buyers of shares believe that the price of a stock underestimates the value of a corporation while sellers of a stock believe that the price of a stock meets or overestimates the value of a corporation. This dynamic is what causes the price of a stock to rise or fall in the market. If there are more buyers than sellers of a stock, the price will go up, if there are more sellers than buyers of a stock, the price will go down.

Despite all the factors that influence stock price, the long-term driver of a corporation's share price is future earnings.

Price to Earnings (P/E) Ratio

The most common method stock investors use to determine a stock's value is by using financial ratios. A ratio compares how much of one thing there is to another. There are many different ratios used to value a stock, depending on the nature of the company's business, the industry it operates in and at what stage the company is in its business life cycle. One of the most common ways of valuing a stock is by using the Price to Earnings (P/E) ratio and comparing it to the P/E ratio of competitors or to the industry in which the company operates. The P/E ratio compares the price of the stock to the company's earnings per share to give you a ratio that you can use to compare to comparable stocks.

The P/E ratio tells you how much an investor is willing to pay for one dollar of future earnings. A P/E ratio of 10 means that an investor is willing to pay $10 for $1 of company earnings.

Why would an investor pay $10 for $1 of earnings? The P/E ratio compares the current price of a stock to its earnings per share in the past year. Because the price of stock is essentially what the investor believes the value of its future earnings will be, an investor is paying for the expected future earnings of the company. The assumption is that a corporation will continue to operate indefinitely into the future and the current price of a stock is the present value of future earnings of the company. Since the market expectations of the future growth of a company is already accounted for in the stock price, the difficult part of stock investing is determining whether you think the current price of a stock is underestimating or overestimating the future earnings of a company.

P/E ratios can differ greatly from industry to industry. As a general rule, mature companies have lower P/E ratios than newer companies that are focused on rapid growth.

The P/E ratio provides an investor with a method to determine a stock's relative value. Let's use the P/E ratios of five Canadian banks to determine which bank may provide the best value.

Table 11 - P/E Ratios of Five Canadian Banks

	TD	BMO	CIBC	BNS	RBC	Industry AVG
Market Cap	84.76B	44.86B	40.30B	69.02B	100.25B	34.10B
P/E	12.64	12.28	13.00	11.41	13.20	13.65
Share Price	$52.72	$79.35	$101.63	$65.07	$79.85	N/A

The banks in the comparison are Toronto Dominion Bank (TD), Bank of Montreal (BMO), Bank of Nova Scotia (BNS), Canadian Imperial Bank of Commerce (CIBC) and Royal Bank (RBC).

The first thing that I would like to point out is that a stock's price is not the best way to determine a company's value. For example, just because CIBC's share price is $101.63 does not mean that CIBC is worth almost twice as much as TD at $52.72. In fact the opposite is true. When we look at the market cap (total value of the company) of both companies; TD's market cap is more than double that of CIBC's. The price of a share is a single piece of information that does not mean much on its own.

One way to compare the difference in stock prices in order to determine which stock may be a good value is to use the P/E ratio. By comparing the P/E ratios of these five banks, the cheapest is Bank of Nova Scotia at a P/E of 11.41 and the most expensive is Royal Bank at a P/E of 13.2. Put another way, based on current market prices, an investor is willing to pay $11.41 for $1 of Bank of Nova Scotia earnings and is willing to pay $13.2 for $1 of Royal Bank earnings. So everything else being equal, a value conscious investor would prefer to buy shares of Bank of Nova Scotia over shares of Royal Bank because the P/E ratio of Bank of Nova Scotia is lower than that of Royal Bank's. You can also compare the P/E ratio of a stock to that of the entire industry to see how the P/E ratio of a company compares to the industry as a whole.

Let's use another example, but this time in the U.S. pharmaceutical industry. The four companies we will compare are Pfizer

(PFE), Merck (MRK), Novartis (NVS) and Sanofi (SNY). Based on the information in table 13, we can see that the P/E ratios of pharmaceutical companies are generally higher than that of the banks we examined earlier. The first thing to note is that the industry as a whole has an average P/E ratio of 24.41 compared to the P/E ratio of the Canadian banking industry at 13.65. The P/E ratios of pharmaceutical companies are higher because investors expect more growth from these companies than they do for banks. This makes sense, since pharmaceutical companies are better able to generate earnings growth by introducing drugs that can grow the company's earnings at a much faster pace than any product a bank can introduce. For that reason, investors are willing to pay a higher P/E ratio for pharmaceutical companies than they would for banks.

Table 12 - P/E Ratios of Four U.S. Pharmaceutical Companies

	PFE	MRK	NVS	SNY	Industry AVG
Market Cap	201.31B	171.08B	228.18B	121.34B	2.09B
P/E	19.71	32.67	21.68	24.18	24.41

Things to Consider When Using P/E Ratios

- P/E ratios are only useful when comparing P/E ratios of companies that operate in similar industries.

- Only companies with profits can be used to compare P/E ratios. Companies that are losing money do not have P/E ratios because they do not have any earnings to compare the share price to.

- Just because a stock has a low P/E ratio does not mean it is a good value. It is a starting point to examine the company in greater detail to find the reasons why it is low and to determine if you think the low P/E ratio is justified.

- The P/E ratio is one tool an investor can use to look for relative value against similar companies.

Importance of Dividends

Over the past 100 years, reinvested dividends have accounted for approximately half of the S&P 500's total return of approximately 17,000% (not adjusted for inflation). During the past 100 years, investing in an index like the S&P 500 has provided investors with an average return of 10-12% over the long- term (not adjusted for inflation).

This does not mean that the market went up 10-12% each and every year, but that over time the average annual return was approximately 10-12%. Approximately half of those gains came from reinvesting the dividends that corporations paid out to shareholders in additional shares of the corporation.

One advantage of dividends is that they act as an excellent buffer against price swings. For example, let's consider two scenarios in which you buy a stock that does not pay a dividend and one in which it does pay a dividend.

Scenario 1: If you buy a stock that costs $100 and then it declines to $90 after one year and pays no dividend, then your investment will have declined by $10.

Scenario 2: Consider if that same stock paid a dividend of $5 per share on an annual basis, then your investment will have only declined by $5. Although the price of the stock declined by $10 over the course of the year, you received a cash dividend payment of $5.

One major advantage that dividend paying stocks have over non-dividend paying stocks is largely psychological in nature. Dividends provide the investor with the psychological comfort that they are receiving a portion of the company's profits on a regular basis. All too often, investors succumb to their emotions when money is involved and sell their investments if they do not appreciate in value quickly.

Human nature often functions in the opposite direction of logic and when people see the value of their investments declining they often panic and sell their investment at a loss only to regret it later when prices recover. Even though the price of your shares may be dropping, you are still earning money with the dividend.

Dividend Dates

When buying the shares of a dividend paying corporation, there are certain dates that relate to the payment of a dividend that an investor needs to be aware of. These are the declaration date, record date, ex-date and payable date.

Declaration date: The date on which the corporation's board of directors declares that a dividend will be paid to common shareholders.

Record date: The date on which shareholders must be recorded as owning shares of the corporation.

Ex-date: The date on which shareholders of the corporation are no longer entitled to the dividend payment promised on the declaration date. On this date, the shares of the corporation exclude the dividend. The ex-date is usually 2 business days before the record date. In order to receive the declared dividend, you must have owned the shares prior to the ex-date.

Payable date: The date on which the dividend is paid.

For example, the following press release was issued on December 3, 2014 by the Royal Bank of Canada.

> *TORONTO, Dec. 3, 2014 - Royal Bank of Canada today announced its quarterly common share dividend of 75 cents per share, payable on February 24, 2015, to common shareholders of record at the close of business on January 30, 2015.*

Declaration date: December 3, 2014

Record date: January 30, 2015

Ex-date: January 28, 2015 (2 business days prior to the record date)

Payable date: February 24, 2015

Based on the above information, in order to receive the declared quarterly dividend on February 24, 2015, you must have been recorded as owning shares of Royal Bank at the close of business on January 30, 2015. The last day that you could purchase Royal Bank shares and be eligible for the declared dividend, would be January 27, 2015. Investors purchasing shares of Royal Bank on or after the ex-date of January 28, 2015 will have to wait until the next quarterly dividend is announced to receive a dividend payment. The reason that the ex-date and record date differ is that a trade takes approximately two days to "settle" meaning that the trade becomes official.

It is important to note that corporations that pay dividends are not under any legal obligation to continue to pay dividends to shareholders in the future. Dividends can be increased, cut or eliminated altogether if management feels it is in the best interests of the company.

One recent example of a corporation suspending their dividend is the Canadian transportation manufacturer, Bombardier. It has paid a dividend to shareholders since 2008 and in February of 2015 management decided that the cash being paid to shareholders would be better used to support its struggling business. This is not to say that Bombardier will never pay a dividend again, only that depending on the nature of the business, some dividends are more consistent than others.

Another example occurred in late 2014 when the price of oil began to plummet from a high of over $100 to below $50 per barrel. Many Canadian oil corporations decided to reduce or eliminate their dividend payments due to the decline in the price of oil.

Some Canadian corporations have consistently maintained and increased their dividends over time regardless of the economic climate. These corporations tend to operate in industries that are more stable and whose cash flow does not depend in large part on the sale of a single product or commodity. These corporations operate in relatively stable industries and have an excellent track record of paying a dividend and increasing it over time. For example:

- Bell Canada Enterprises
- Telus Communications
- Bank of Montreal
- Royal Bank of Canada
- Toronto Dominion Bank
- Canadian Imperial Bank of Commerce
- Sun Life Financial
- Canadian National Railway
- Great West Life Co.
- Shaw Communications

Risk

When someone says the word "risk", what comes to mind?

In our day-to-day lives the notion of risk usually implies the possibility of loss or injury and should be avoided. It carries a purely negative connotation so it is difficult to think of risk in any other way, including investment risk.

When most people think about stocks, one of the first things that come to mind is risk.

Investment risk is different than the risk of daily life because there is a potential for reward for the risk you are taking. Risk in your daily life, like the potential of your house burning down or getting hit by a bus, provide no potential upside. Investment risk, on the other hand, is unique in that the riskier an investment is, the higher the potential for reward.

If we use the conventional definition of risk (the possibility of loss), then a Canada Savings Bond that pays an annual 0.5% interest yield is less risky than shares of Bell Canada that pay a 5% annual dividend yield. There is virtually no chance of a loss on Canada Savings Bonds and because Bell Canada is a corporation that has the potential for a share price decline, it carries a higher degree of risk. Using our knowledge of inflation, let's use an example to see which investment is really riskier.

Scenario 1 – GICs

Let's assume you have $10,000 to invest and have an investment time frame of five years. Because you do not want any "risk", you decide to buy a GIC and hold it for five years. The interest rate offered on the GIC is 0.5% and the annual inflation rate is 2%.

After five years, you will get $10,000 back and $250 of interest. On the surface, it appears that you successfully avoided any risk and made $250 while getting your principal back. However, a deeper analysis reveals something different. When we adjust for the 2% inflation, the $10,000 you get back will now only be worth $9,057.31.

	Inflation Adjusted Value of Principal
At the Start	$10,000.00
End of Year 1	$9,803.92
End of Year 2	$9,611.69
End of Year 3	$9,423.22
End of Year 4	$9,238.45
End of Year 5	$9,057.31

The annual 0.5% interest payments amount to $240.38 when adjusted for inflation:

	Annual Interest	Inflation Adjusted Interest
Year 1	$50.00	$46.19
Year 2	$50.00	$47.17
Year 3	$50.00	$48.06
Year 4	$50.00	$49.02
Year 5	$50.00	$50.00
Total	$250.00	$240.38

Adding up these values we obtain a total real investment value of $9,297.69. Or put another way, a loss of $702.31 (7.02%)! This seemingly "safe" investment with no "risk" led to a pretty substantial loss.

Scenario 2 – Bell Canada Shares

Instead, imagine you choose a "risky" stock investment and buy $10,000 of Bell Canada shares and hold them for five years.

Let's assume that you buy 200 shares at $50 each for a total investment of $10,000 and the shares pay an annual dividend of $2.50 per share for a 5% dividend yield ($2.50/$50). Also let's say that Bell Canada increases its dividend by 2% annually.

Note that the actual annual dividend for 2014 was $2.47 and for 2015 was $2.60. In addition, Bell has increased its dividend by over 5% per year for the past five years. So the assumptions here are both realistic and conservative.

	Annual Dividend	Inflation Adjusted Dividend
Year 1	$500.00	$461.92
Year 2	$510.00	$480.48
Year 3	$520.00	$499.81
Year 4	$530.00	$519.61
Year 5	$540.00	$540.00
Total	$2,600.00	$2,501.82

Your inflation-adjusted dividend payments will give you $2,501.82 over five years. If we assume the value of the shares remain at $50, your total real investment value is $12,501.82

The above examples are meant to demonstrate that the concept of investment risk must be looked at in the context of total inflation adjusted returns. Given the fact that "safe" investments such as savings accounts and GICs do not pay enough interest to even keep up with inflation, they are essentially guaranteed to lose money over time.

People tend to paint all stocks with the same wide brush strokes, using comments such as the 'market casino' or 'playing' the stock market. This implies that that the stock market and the stocks that trade on them are meaningless pieces of paper that can be worth a large sum one minute and nothing the next. It is true that stocks can experience wide fluctuations in price, but one important thing to remember is that over time, the returns from "risky" investments such as stocks with far outperform the returns from "safe" investments like savings accounts and GICs.

Interested in Buying Individual Stocks?

If you are interested in buying individual stocks, I highly suggest setting up a practice account and not to trade with real money for at least one year while you further educate yourself on how the stock market works in more detail.

I suggest following at least five stocks for one year to get a good sense of how and why prices of stocks move the way they do.

Here are some questions to help you find stocks to follow in your practice account:

- Who is your bank?
- Who is your mobile service provider?
- Who is your insurance company?
- What make of car do you drive?

- What social media networks do you use?

- What stores do you shop at?

- Who owns the apartment building you live in?

- Who do you have your mortgage with?

- Who makes your toothpaste?

For example:

- Who is your bank? **Bank of Montreal**

- Who makes your toothpaste? **Procter and Gamble** owns the Crest brand

- What social media networks do you use? **Facebook, Twitter, Pinterest**

- Who is your mobility service provider? **Telus**

- Who is your insurance company? **Sun Life Financial**

Once you have answered these questions, go to the company's website and find the Investor Relations section if they have one. If the company is not publicly traded then the company will not have an Investor Relations website. Here you will find excellent information about the company, its strategy, its ticker symbol and dividends. You may want to do this for one of the example companies that you listed above, say Telus.

Income Trusts

Income trusts are companies that own various income producing assets or businesses. Income trusts trade on stock exchanges just like common shares of corporations and can increase or decrease in price over time. The pieces of ownership are called units instead of shares.

The objective of income trusts is to pay unit holders a steady stream of income on what is usually a monthly basis. Income trusts pay out a high portion, usually 70% or more of their earnings to unit holders in the form of a monthly distribution, which are similar to dividends. Distributions are often taxed differently than dividends (more on this below).

Income trusts are particularly attractive for investors who are looking for a stable monthly cash flow. Income trusts usually consist of mature businesses that provide a high level of earnings. They offer relatively high annual distribution yields of between 4-8%, compared to common stocks that pay between 2-4% annual dividend yields.

Real Estate Investment Trusts (REITs) are income trusts that own real estate assets like residential or office buildings. They are the most popular form of income trust because of the stability and predictability of cash flows that they offer.

Since trusts are usually mature businesses that pay out the majority of their earnings to unit holders, they usually do not experience the volatility in unit price that common stocks do.

There are approximately 200 income trusts in Canada, many of which offer sustainable, recurring, high yield cash flow. Some examples of income trusts include apartment buildings, office buildings, retirement homes, energy trusts, mortgage corporations, and many more.

Here are a few of the most popular REITs in Canada:

- **Riocan REIT** – The largest REIT in Canada by market cap. It owns shopping centers in Canada and the U.S.

- **Canadian Apartment Properties REIT** – The largest owner of apartment properties in Canada.

- **Smart REIT** – Primarily owns Wal-Mart occupied properties.

- **Northwest Healthcare Properties** – The largest owner of healthcare related properties in Canada such as clinics and doctor's offices.

- **Chartwell Retirement Residences** – One of Canada's largest owner/operators of retirement homes.

Income trusts are not without risk. Like any business, income trusts can experience economic downturns or poor management, leading to a decline in the value of the business or a reduction or elimination of the distribution. Income trusts are also sensitive to interest rates and can experience fluctuations in price during periods of volatility in interest rates. Due to usually high debt levels, rises in interest rates are seen as negative for income trusts. In general, an increase in interest rates will decrease the price of an income trust and vice-versa.

While income trusts are usually considered more suitable to older investors who wish to receive an income stream in retirement, they do offer some unique opportunities for millennial investors as well. They offer the opportunity for excellent returns over time by reinvesting the monthly distributions into more units of the trust to compound returns over time.

Taxation of Income Trusts

If a unit of a trust is sold at a profit, normal capital gains taxation would apply in the same way it is applied to common shares.

Distributions from income trusts are taxed differently from dividends. Most distributions are taxed as a 'Return of Capital' which is generally not taxable when it is received. It is as if the company is giving you your money (capital) back during each distribution. However, those distributions reduce the cost of your original investment. So when you sell the units, even if the price did not increase, you may earn a capital gain.

For example, let's assume you buy 1000 units at $10 per unit ($10,000) of a REIT that pays a monthly distribution of $0.04167 per unit for an annual distribution yield of 5%. In one year, you will have received 12 payments of $41.67 for a total of $500. Let's also assume that the price of the units remains the same and one year later you decide to sell the units for the same $10 you paid for them. At first glance it may not seem that you will have to pay a capital gain, but the distributions you received reduced your cost by $500. For taxation purposes, it is as if you paid $9,500 for your shares and then sold them for $10,000 triggering a capital gain of $500.

It is important to note that distributions can be a mix of various types of taxable income. It is not uncommon for a distribution to be made up of a mix of capital gains, interest, return of capital, or other types of income, which are all taxed differently. Before purchasing any income trust, it is first important to understand what the makeup of the distribution is. This information can be found on the Investor Relations page of the website of the trust and you should consult a qualified tax professional for a complete understanding of how distributions will be taxed.

Dividend/Distribution Reinvestment Plans (DRIPs)

Dividend/Distribution Reinvestment Plans (DRIPs) allow for an investor to receive additional shares/units of their investment without paying any commissions. They are an excellent way for the shareholder or unitholder to increase their ownership in a dividend/distribution paying corporation, trust or Exchange Traded Fund (ETF) without incurring any brokerage charges or commissions. Some companies offer investors incentives to enroll in the DRIP such as a discounts or bonuses on the new shares issued.

For example, let's assume you own 1000 units of a REIT that operates apartment buildings across North America and the price of the units are $10 for a total investment of $10,000. The REIT pays a monthly distribution of $0.05 per unit for an annual distribution yield of 6%. For your $10,000 investment you will receive $50 in distributions each month (1000 units x $0.05). You have little need for investment income at this point in your life, so you elect to enroll your units in the REIT's DRIP program. Each month, the distribution is used to purchase additional units in the trust at no cost. At the end of the first month of ownership, instead of receiving $50 deposited into the account in which the units are held, your account will be credited with an additional five units ($50 ÷ $10/unit) and you will own 1005 units.

To demonstrate the power of compounding distributions over time, let's assume you hold the units for 30 years, allowing the distributions to be continually reinvested. Further assume the units stay at the same price of $10 per unit and there is a full reinvestment of distributions.

	Units	Value	Monthly Distribution
End of Year 1	1056	$10,563.96	$52.82
End of Year 2	1122	$11,215.52	$56.08
End of Year 3	1191	$11,907.27	$59.54
End of Year 4	1264	$12,641.68	$63.21
End of Year 5	1342	$13,421.39	$67.11
...	...	...	...
End of Year 10	1810	$18,103.45	$90.52
...	...	...	...
End of Year 20	3294	$32,927.36	$164.69
...	...	...	...
End of Year 30	5993	$59,926.12	$299.63

Your $10,000 investment will have grown to almost $60,000 in 30 years, and will pay you an income of nearly $300 per month. Not only will you have achieved a 16.67% annual growth rate of because of compounded returns (with no unit price appreciation), if you choose to terminate your participation in the DRIP and start receiving cash payments, you will receive a $300 monthly income in retirement.

DRIP Enrollment

There are two main types of DRIPs: "Traditional" DRIP and a "Synthetic" DRIP. The traditional DRIP is offered by the company and administered by a Transfer Agent. A Transfer Agent is a company acting on behalf of the dividend/distribution paying company to administer its DRIP program. In order to enroll in a DRIP you must fill out a form available on the Transfer Agent website and mail it along with a cheque to purchase shares in the company at no cost.

The advantage of a traditional DRIP is that you can purchase company shares/units without paying any commissions. Some DRIPs have a minimum number of shares that an investor must own in order to be enrolled, while others do not have a minimum and allow for fractional shares (less than one unit) to be reinvested.

The disadvantage of traditional DRIPs is that they cannot be administered in registered accounts such as RRSPs or TFSAs, therefore dividends/distributions are subject to taxation. Another drawback is that when shares are initially purchased, you have no control over what price you pay for the shares.

In order to enroll in a DRIP, you must first see if the company/fund offers one by visiting the company or ETF's website. For synthetic DRIPs, some discount brokers have lists of eligible securities that can be enrolled in a DRIP. Just because a company or ETF offers a DRIP does not necessarily mean that your broker will have it as one of their DRIP eligible investments. In order to enroll in a DRIP, contact your broker and request that your shares/units be enrolled in the DRIP program.

Whole and Fractional Shares

Synthetic DRIP programs require that only whole shares can be purchased and that any remaining fractional units be paid in cash.

Let's use the previous example of your $10,000 investment in which you own 1000 units of a REIT for $10 per unit that pays a monthly distribution of $0.05 per unit for an annual yield of 6%. Assume this REIT offers a DRIP program, but only allows for the reinvestment of whole units.

Your 1000 units will yield $50 in distributions each month (1000 units x $0.05). At the end of the first month, the $50 you received as a distribution will be reinvested by purchasing an additional five units of the REIT (assuming the price of the units have remained constant at $10).

The following month, you will own 1005 units that will pay you a distribution of $50.25 (1005 x $0.05). However, the full $50.25 will not be able to be reinvested because the maximum number of whole units that can be purchased is five (assuming the price of the units have remained at $10). The remaining $0.25 will be deposited as cash in the account in which the units are held.

Compound Interest and DRIPs

The simple idea of interest earned on an investment being reinvested to earn more interest over time can produce powerful returns over time. But don't just take my word on it; here is what Einstein and Warren Buffet have to say:

> *"The power of compound interest the most powerful force in the universe."*
> — Albert Einstein

> *"My wealth has come from a combination of living in America, some lucky genes, and compound interest."*
> — Warren Buffett

One of the most powerful investing lessons I ever learned was the seemingly magic power of compound interest. If you leave your money in an interest bearing account long enough and let the interest accumulate to earn more interest, you will double your money over time, depending on the interest rate.

A simple way of determining how long your investment will take to double is known as the 'Rule of 72'. Simply divide 72 by the interest rate on your investments and you will receive a fairly accurate number of years that it will take your investment to double. For example, an investment of $10,000 earning 2% interest will take approximately 72 / 2 = 36 years to double, while a $10,000 investment earning 8% interest will take approximately 72 / 8 = 9 years to double.

The ability to compound returns is not limited to interest earning instruments like GICs and bonds. Equity investments such as stocks and income trusts can also be compounded to produce even more powerful results over time, through participating in DRIPs.

Mutual Funds

A *mutual fund* is an investment fund that pools individual investor money and is managed by one or more fund managers. An individual piece of the fund is known as a unit and does not trade on a stock exchange. Fund managers invest the money in stocks, bonds, GICs, indexes or many other combinations of investments. Mutual funds are sold by all the major banks, insurance companies and other investment dealers and charge various fees for the management of the funds.

Why Buy a Mutual Fund?

Mutual funds are attractive to investors for the convenience and diversification they provide. Investors with little to no knowledge of investments who want someone else managing their money often choose mutual funds. These investors expect that the fund will produce a better return than if they invest their money themselves or not at all.

Table 13 - The Main Types of Mutual Funds

Type of Fund	Invests In
Money Market	Short-term Cash Equivalent Investments
Fixed Income	Government and Corporate Bonds
Growth/Equity	Stocks
Index	Major Market Indexes Such as TSX, Dow, S&P 500
Specialty	Specific Region or Sector
Balanced	Combination of Any of the Above Types

Mutual Fund Fees

The most important thing to understand about mutual funds is that they are products being sold by an institution whose primary goal is to make a profit. The way banks or investment companies make money is by charging investors sales charges, fees, and expenses to manage the fund. The top charges are Sales Charges which are also known as 'Loads' and Management Expense Ratio fees (MER).

Sales Charges (Loads)

An investor may have to pay a sales charge when they buy or sell units of a fund. Mutual funds can have a front-end load, back-end load, low load or no load.

- **Front-end Load** – This is a commission, usually a percentage of between (0-5%) of your total investment in the fund. This is also known sometimes as an 'Initial Sales Charge'. It is paid when you purchase the fund.

- **Back-end Load** – This is a commission, usually a percentage between (0-6%), that a fund will charge when you sell units of the fund. This is also known as a 'Deferred Sales Charge'. Generally, the longer you hold the fund, the lower the charge will be or there will be no charge at all.

- **Low Load** – These are mutual funds that charge a lower Front-end or Back-end load.

- **No load** – No fees are charged when you buy or sell units of the mutual fund.

Management Expense Ratio (MER)

All mutual funds have MER fees. The MER is charged as a percentage of your total investment in a fund. It is paid annually to the managers of the fund for the service of managing the investments and their operating expenses. MERs usually range anywhere between 1-3%. These fees are paid regardless of whether the fund makes or loses money.

The individual investor in the mutual fund does not pay these fees directly, but rather they are subtracted from the value of the fund. For example, if you own a mutual fund for one year that grew by 5% that has a MER of 2%, your gain will be 3%. Although you personally did not have to pay the MER of 2%, it did reduce your total gain by 2%. Similarly, if you owned a fund that depreciated by 5%, with a MER of 2%, the total decline in your investment would be 7%.

Let's do an example to demonstrate the impact of MERs over time. A 2% MER may not sound like much, but with the power of compounding over time, it can add up to be quite significant.

Imagine you make an initial investment of $10,000 at age 30 and invest $5,000 a year for the next 25 years in a mutual fund with an average annual return of 10% with a MER of 2%.

In 25 years, at age 55, your investment will have grown to a total value of $595,082.36. However, the MER of 2% compounded over 25 years has cost you $98,711.36 in fees. Put another way, had you not been paying a 2% MER for 25 years and that money was instead working for you, you would have had an additional $155,268.73 at the end of 25 years due to the effects of compounding. You can find a helpful mutual fund fee calculator on the website: www.getsmarteraboutmoney.ca

Financial Advisors

Mutual funds are usually sold by financial advisors who work largely on commission. On the next page is an actual job description for a financial advisor position at an investment firm. Take a moment to read it through.

For a job in which you would think your primary role would be to provide advice regarding someone's finances, the job description on the following page is more of a sales pitch for building your own wealth and not that of your clients. In fact, you don't even need a finance background, but as long as you can sell, you're hired.

Position Summary: Individuals from a variety of occupational backgrounds, including salespeople, I.T. professionals and corporate managers, have found new success at Corporation ABC. Here is your chance to train and become licensed in a high-growth industry while running a business in your community, all with no upfront investment or franchise fee required. By becoming a Corporation ABC Financial Advisor, you can run your business, determine your compensation and redefine your future.

As a Financial Advisor, you have the opportunity to*:

- *Build a business from an office in your community making face-to-face contacts in neighborhoods and with businesses*
- *Cultivate and get to know clients, their investment needs and their objectives in order to deliver appropriate investments and services*
- *Receive in-depth financial and business development training*
- *Earn commissions, bonuses, profit sharing and incentive travel*
- *Apply a proven business model*
- *Earn a full-time branch office assistant who manages client service and marketing activities*
- *Earn partnership in the firm*

Qualities that help you succeed:

- *A solid sales or management history (although not necessary)*
- *The commitment and relationship-building skills crucial to establishing long-term clients*
- *A strong desire to work on commissions for unlimited earning potential*
- *The ability to be highly driven, sales-oriented and self-managing*
- *The desire and capacity to work autonomously from an office in your community*

Financial advisors will justify their fees as 'paying for performance' and show you how the fund has outperformed various benchmarks and indexes in the past. Although it may be true that a fund has outperformed some benchmark of similar investments for a period of time in the past, that is no guarantee that they will continue to do so in the future.

In fact, research has shown that between 80-95% of mutual fund managers do not consistently beat the broad market indexes like the S&P 500 based on superior market-timing or stock-picking skills.

The problem is not that fund managers are not skilled at picking great stocks and knowing when to buy them. Rather, the problem is that the profits are eaten up by trading costs and management fees. This means that excellent fund managers and their firms keep the fruits of their outperformance, usually leaving investors with a market return at best. However, the fact remains that many actively managed mutual funds still don't outperform the market, even before fees are subtracted.

If you choose to work with a Financial Advisor, be sure to know what the fund invests in, what the goals of the fund are and what fees are being charged.

So what to do if you're not conformable selecting your own investments and you don't feel comfortable paying the fees that mutual funds charge? The Exchange Traded Fund (ETF) is probably the best financial innovation of the past 20 years and may be right for you.

Exchange Traded Funds (ETFs)

Exchange Traded Funds (ETFs) are traded like stocks with the diversification of a mutual fund at a much lower MER.

ETFs trade on stock exchanges just like common shares or trusts. They can be purchased by individuals through their investment brokerage account. Like mutual funds, ETFs can hold a basket of investments in various sectors like banking, energy, real estate.

They can also mirror the performance of an index like the S&P 500.

Let's compare a mutual fund and an ETF with similar investment objectives. Let's compare a TD mutual fund (TD Dividend Income Fund) with iShares Canadian Select Dividend Index ETF.

		TD Dividend Income Fund	iShares Canadian Select Dividend Index ETF
MER		2.03%	0.55%
Top 5 Fund Holdings	1	TD Bank	CIBC
	2	Royal Bank	TD Bank
	3	CIBC	National Bank
	4	Bank of NS	BMO
	5	BMO	Royal Bank
5 Year Annual Return (net of fees) as of Nov 30, 2014		9.32%	11.23%

As you can see with the above comparative analysis, the holdings are very similar, but what stands out is the difference in the MER and total return. The difference in MERs can produce a large discrepancy in returns due to the effects of compounding.

For example, imagine you make an initial investment of $10,000 at age 30 in both of these funds and you make annual contributions of $5,000 for the next 25 years. In 25 years, by investing in the ETF with a MER of 0.55% as opposed to the mutual fund MER at 2.03%, you will have saved $61,461.24 in fees and made an additional $198,617.30.

	Mutual Fund	**ETF**
Average Return	9.32%	11.23%
Return After Fees	$401,927.95	$600,454.25
Final Investment Value	$531,927.95	$730,545.25

Costs	Mutual Fund	ETF
MER	$92,615.48	$31,154.24
MER (%)	2.04%	0.55%

Below is a list of some ETF providers in Canada:

- Vanguard Investments Canada:
  https://www.vanguardcanada.ca/individual/etfs.htm

- Blackrock (iShares) Canada:
  http://www.blackrock.com/ca/

- Bank of Montreal ETFs:
  http://www.etfs.bmo.com/

- RBC ETFs:
  http://funds.rbcgam.com/etfs/

- TD e-Series Funds:
  https://www.tdcanadatrust.com/products-services/investing/mutual-funds/td-eseries-funds.jsp

Where to Find Investment Ideas

Believe it or not, investment ideas are all around you. If you develop the mindset of an investor you'll see opportunities everywhere. You'll quickly realize that the possibilities within the global economy are seemingly endless. So where to start?

Begin by following the stocks or units of companies that you are familiar with. Select those in which you understand on a basic level how the business operates. Ask yourself the same questions listed in the section on common stocks on pages 102-103.

Check out their websites and find the 'Investor Relations' page for investor presentations, annual reports, share price information and more.

From the novice to the more experienced investor, it is important to know what you are investing in. If you cannot explain how a company makes money in two sentences or less, maybe you shouldn't be investing in it.

Investing/personal finance magazines such as MoneySense often have excellent articles on various topics ranging from personal finance, taxes and investments. The TV channel Business News Network (BNN) also provides viewers with excellent information on the world of finance and investment. Guests on the show explain financial concepts to viewers in a manner that they can understand.

I am an avid watcher of BNN, in particular the call-in show *Market Call*. Viewers call-in or email questions to guests who have in-depth knowledge of various market industries and ask for their recommendations. By watching the show, I discovered many investments that I didn't even know existed which are now in my investment portfolio.

Once you've come up with a list of stocks, trusts or ETFs that interest you, set up a free "practice portfolio" where you can buy and sell these stocks, units and ETFs NOT using real money. Most discount brokers offer free practice accounts. You can also set up a free practice account on sites such as Google or Yahoo! Finance.

By setting up a practice account, you can observe how the prices of shares, units or ETFs react in the market. This will give you a sense of how prices move and why. Gaining a basic understanding of how everything works before committing real investment dollars is a valuable lesson and time well spent.

Now that you have an idea of what your investment options are you must be wondering how to get started. The following section will help you get started by showing you how to set a goal, make a plan and take action.

PART 5: TAKING ACTION

Given in the inadequacy of the CPP and OAS to provide for all your financial needs in retirement, the need to start investing to supplement your retirement is vital.

As you've already seen, the earlier you start investing the better. The advantage that millennials have is time. By setting a goal, making a plan and sticking to it, you can build enough wealth to retire on your own terms.

You can achieve this in various ways, such as using a financial advisor, managing your own portfolio or using an all-in-one portfolio.

But first, let's start by setting a goal.

HOW MUCH MONEY WILL YOU NEED IN RETIREMENT?

The amount of money someone will need in retirement can vary greatly from person to person. Some retirees can live comfortably with a reduction of between 50-70% of their pre-retirement income, while others cannot.

Some retirees see their living expenses decrease due to their mortgages being paid off and the children having moved out. Others will still need a high percentage of pre-retirement income for long-term care or similar living expenses.

I believe it is always better to "have more than you need" rather than to "need more than you have". I have never heard anyone regret that they saved too much for retirement.

Setting a Goal

Let's start with a simple example and assume your annual income is $48,250. Using this information, let's imagine that you are a 22-year-old Ontario resident that plans to retire at age 65. For simplicity, let's assume your salary increases at the same rate as inflation. You would like to have at least $40,000 per year in retirement income to live comfortably. Based on the average salary of $48,250, when you retire at 65 you can expect to receive approximately:

Monthly Pension: CPP + OAS: $900 + $565 =	$1,465.00
Annual Pension: $1,465.00 x 12 =	**$17,580.00**

Based on the combined amounts from CPP and OAS, if you do not save anything to supplement your income, you will experience a shortfall of $22,420 ($40,000 -$ 17,580) per year. Your goal therefore becomes to generate enough wealth to receive at least $22,420 in annual income from your investments.

One Goal, Different Ways to Get There

One approach to building enough wealth to obtain $22,420 in annual income would be to build enough retirement savings in order to slowly deplete the savings over time and live off the principal and interest payments.

This approach focuses on growing retirement savings and then once the desired amount is reached, placing the principal in a GIC or savings bond and depleting the funds over time.

This is essentially how RRSPs function because when you are forced to convert your RRSP into a RRIF, you must withdraw a certain minimum per year. For example, if you plan to retire at 65 and assume you will live until 87 (in 2012, the average life expectancy in Canada was 80.4 for a male and 84.6 for a female), you would need $448,400 (20 x $22,420) to have 20 years' worth of income using the interest payments to keep up with inflation.

This approach is fraught with problems because there is the possibility of outliving your assets. What if you live to 90? What if you live to 100? Conversely, what if you die at 70 with $400,000 in an RRSP or RRIF with no eligible dependents to transfer the money to? The $400,000 will be taxed at your marginal rate and in some provinces about half of the money will be lost in taxes!

If you are uncomfortable with the idea of possibly outliving your assets, you may want to consider the approach of building a portfolio from which you can receive investment income without depleting your principal.

Let's assume that you can earn a 4% yield from a portfolio of dividend/distribution paying stocks and income trusts. In order to calculate the amount needed for you to receive $22,420 and not deplete your principal, you would divide the annual income needed by the yield on your investments:

Principal Required: $22,420 ÷ 4% =	$560,500

As you can see, you will need $560,500, in order to generate a $22,420 income without depleting your principal.

MAKING A PLAN

As a general rule, many financial experts and pundits say that you should 'pay yourself first'; a phrase originally coined by George S. Clason in his book *The Richest Man in Babylon* and save at least 10% of your pay.

For example, let's assume you are 22 and based on a salary of $48,250, you would receive approximately $1,400 every two weeks after taxes and deductions. Ten percent (10%) of $1,400 is $140. Let's further assume you would like to amass $560,500 by the age of 65. Since you are 22 and have 43 years to achieve this amount, what inflation-adjusted rate of return will you need to achieve your goal?

Based on data from 1934 to 2015, Table 14 presents the historical returns of several investments:

Table 14 - Historic Returns of Different Investments

Investments	Annualized Return	Inflation-adjusted Return (3.7%)
U.S. Stocks	11.1%	7.4%
Canadian Stocks	9.9%	6.1%
Balanced Portfolio (50% Stocks, 50% Bonds)	8.6%	5.0%
International Stocks (excluding U.S.)	8.3%	4.6%
Bonds	6.2%	2.5%
GICs	4.6%	0.9%

The above table is only meant to demonstrate how these different investments have performed in the past, and what can be reasonably expected in the future.

Using this information, you can now begin to make a plan on how to achieve your goal of amassing $560,500 in retirement savings.

Let's assume you decide to invest in a balanced portfolio consisting of 50% stocks and 50% bonds. Using the above historical data you assume an inflation-adjusted return of 5%. How much will you need to save every pay to reach $560,500 in retirement savings?

Using the Financial Consumer Agency of Canada's Retirement Calculator, you will need to save a minimum of $129.63 every two weeks in order to achieve this goal. Since you are contributing 10% of your salary or $140 every two weeks, if you stick to the plan then you should have no problem achieving your goal.

What if you did not want any stocks in your investment portfolio? You would then have to assume a lower rate of return, but how would this affect the amount you have to save? If you have all bonds in your portfolio and assume an inflation adjusted return of 2.5%, then you would have to save $252.47 every two weeks. Since you are contributing only $140 every two weeks and because of the lower expected rate of return from an all bonds portfolio, you will have to contribute an *extra* $112.47 every two weeks in order to achieve your goal.

The Financial Consumer Agency of Canada's Retirement Calculator can be found at their website.

BENEFITS OF REGULAR CONTRIBUTIONS

The main benefits of making regular contributions are that you are automating your savings and using the concept of dollar-cost averaging. *Dollar-cost averaging* is a technique of making regular fixed contributions to an investment. By making regular fixed contributions, you are buying more of the investment when it is low and less of it when it is high. For example, let's assume your New Year's resolution is to begin making automated regular monthly contributions of $100 to the fictional investment fund 'ABC' to begin saving for retirement.

Over the course of one year, you will make 12 x $100 contributions for an annual contribution of $1,200. You begin your new investment regime with excitement and buy $100 worth of ABC fund for $12, but after one month, you notice the fund has decreased in value to $11 and the month after to $10. You begin to get nervous and start questioning yourself.

You remember the concept of dollar-cost averaging and make the decision to stick with your plan and continue making regular contributions. The fund reaches a low of $7 in June and July and you are so distraught that you stop looking at your monthly statement. You forget about your investment, and slowly the fund recovers in price to $12 by the end of the year. You open your annual statement expecting the worst, but notice that your total investment is worth $1,587 even though you contributed $1,200 ($100 per month). You believe it must be a mistake and look at your statement more closely.

You notice that by making regular contributions you were able to buy less of the fund when it was high and more of it when it was low. In fact, the average price you paid for the units was $9.07 ($1,200/ 132.28):

Month	Contribution	Price	Units
JAN	$100	$12	8.33
FEB	$100	$11	9.91
MAR	$100	$10	10
APR	$100	$9	11.11
MAY	$100	$8	15.5
JUN	$100	$7	14.29
JUL	$100	$7	14.29
AUG	$100	$8	12.50
SEP	$100	$9	11.11
OCT	$100	$10	10
NOV	$100	$11	9.91
DEC	$100	$12	8.33
	Units		132.28
	Value		$1,587.36

There are different ways to go about making a retirement plan. You can work with a financial advisor or invest on your own. Investing on your own involves either designing and building your own investment portfolio or using an all-in-one portfolio.

WAYS TO MAKE A PLAN

Working With a Financial Advisor

The advantage of working with a financial advisor is that you have someone to guide you through the process of planning your retirement. It requires very little involvement on your part and gives you face to face time, which allows you to ask questions and may provide you with peace of mind over your investments. This approach also allows you to 'pay yourself first' and make regular contributions. The advisor should also meet with you at least once a year to discuss the portfolio and make any changes if necessary.

The disadvantage of working with an advisor is that for the most part, their compensation is tied to the investment products they sell you. And these often carry high MER fees that can eat up a large part of your investment returns over time. If you do choose to use an advisor, you may want to strongly insist on using ETFs if possible.

Going It on Your Own

If you've made the decision to manage your own investment portfolio, you will need to set up a trading account at an investment broker. As I mentioned before, there are full service brokers and discount brokers.

Full service brokers require you to call during trading hours on business days and ask that a broker place a trade for you. Full service brokers can be quite expensive, with most charging commissions of over $50 a trade.

Discount brokers are much less expensive and trades can be placed online at a much lower cost, usually between $5-$10 per trade. Below is a list of some of the major discount brokerages in Canada and their cost per trade that is current at the time of writing, but may have changed since, so visit the broker website for the most current information:

- Investorline (BMO): $9.95

- iTrade (Scotia): $9.99

- Webroker (TD): $9.95

- Direct Invest (RBC): $9.95

- Investor's Edge (CIBC): $5.95

- Questrade: $4.95

- Wealthsimple Trade: Free

Some discount brokers charge fees for having an account. These fees are usually referred to as maintenance fees, account inactivity fees or administration fees. These fees are usually about $25 per quarter, but can be waived if you complete a minimum number of trades per quarter or maintain a minimum account balance. It is important to know about these fees, especially if you are just starting out and do not have a high account balance.

Brokers give you access to all the major North American (Canada and U.S.) exchanges and give you the ability to buy the shares, units and ETFs that trade on them. They also provide investment research, tutorials on how to use their services, educational resources such as webinars and many other great tools to improve your investment knowledge.

Designing and Building Your Portfolio

An investment portfolio is a collection of investment assets such as stocks, bonds, mutual funds or ETFs. *Asset allocation* is the mix of investments in a portfolio. Investment portfolios are designed based on your age, investment goals and tolerance for risk. There is no one correct way to design your portfolio, but one aspect of portfolio design that is universally agreed upon is the importance of diversification. *Diversification* is the idea of spreading your investments around so that you are not overly exposed to one particular asset class.

Traditional portfolios usually consist of a mix of equities (stocks and trusts) and fixed income (bonds and GICs) with the equity portion of your portfolio decreasing as you age. The idea behind this is that because equities are viewed as riskier than fixed income, as you age you have less time to make up any decline in equities. In addition, the value of stocks and bonds are historically negatively correlated, so that when stocks perform well, bonds perform less well and vice versa. A common rule of thumb is that your age is the percentage of your portfolio that should be in fixed income. For example, if you are 30, then 30% of your portfolio should be in fixed income investments:

Age	Equities	Fixed Income
30	70%	30%
50	50%	50%
70	30%	70%

This is only a rule of thumb meant to demonstrate the basic concept of portfolio allocation. Most discount brokers and ETF providers have web resources on designing your portfolio.

Portfolio Reallocation

Reallocation or rebalancing your portfolio, is the process of adjusting your portfolio based on your desired asset allocation. For example, let's assume it is January 1, 2015, you are 50, you have a portfolio of $100,000 and you wish to maintain a portfolio allocation of 50% in equities and 50% in fixed income:

	Equities	Fixed Income
Jan 1, 2015 ($100,000)	$50,000	$50,000
Allocation	50%	50%

After approximately one year, on December 31, 2015 the equity portion increases from $50,000 to $65,000 and the fixed income portfolio declines from $50,000 to $45,000. You are pleased that the total value of your portfolio has increased to $110,000, but you have noticed that your portfolio allocation is no longer 50% in equities and 50% in fixed income. More specifically, the equity portion of your portfolio is now 59% ($65,000/$110,000) and the fixed income portion is now 41%:

	Equities	Fixed Income
Dec 31, 2015 ($110,000)	$65,000	$45,000
Allocation	59%	41%

In order to maintain your desired portfolio allocation, you sell $10,000 of equities and purchase $10,000 of fixed income to bring your portfolio back into balance:

	Equities	Fixed Income
Jan 1, 2016 ($110,000)	$55,000	$55,000
Allocation	50%	50%

Portfolio reallocation is important to maintain your desired asset allocation with the added benefit of selling assets when they are high and buying other assets when they are low.

Designing Your Portfolio Using ETFs

Below is a list of ETFs for your consideration. This is not an exhaustive list or a recommendation, but a starting point to ETF investing. ETFs with the lowest MERs are those that track an index such as the TSX Composite Index or the S&P 500:

U.S. Stocks

	Symbol	MER
Vanguard S&P 500 ETF	VGG	0.08%
BMO S&P 500 ETF	ZSP	0.10%

Canadian Stocks

	Symbol	MER
iShares TSX Composite	XIC	0.05%
Vanguard FTSE Canada	VCE	0.05%

International Stocks

	Symbol	MER
BMO MSCI EAFE	ZEA	0.20%
Vanguard FTSE Developed ex North America	VDU	0.20%

Bonds

	Symbol	MER
BMO Aggregate Bond Index	ZAG	0.23%
iShares High Quality Canadian Bond	XQB	0.12%
Vanguard Canadian Aggregate Bond Index	VAB	0.12%

Dividend Stocks

	Symbol	MER
iShares Core S&P/TSX Composite High Dividend Index	XEI	0.20%
FTSE Canadian High Dividend Yield Index	VDY	0.20%

Example of Designing Your Own Portfolio with ETFs

Let's say you have $10,000 to invest and would like 70% in equities and 30% in bonds. Using your discount brokerage, you deposit $10,000 to fund your account. Thinking about portfolio allocation, you can design your portfolio as follows.

You split the equity portion, with half being in Canadian stocks and the other half being in U.S. stocks. For the bond portion of your portfolio you decide to hold only Canadian bonds. You look

for the lowest cost ETFs and select the iShares Core S&P/TSX
Capped Composite Index ETF with a MER of 0.05% for your Canadian equity component. For the U.S. equity component, you
choose the Vanguard S&P 500 Index ETF with a MER of 0.08%
and for your fixed income component, you choose the Vanguard
Canadian Aggregate Bond Index ETF with a MER of 0.12%.

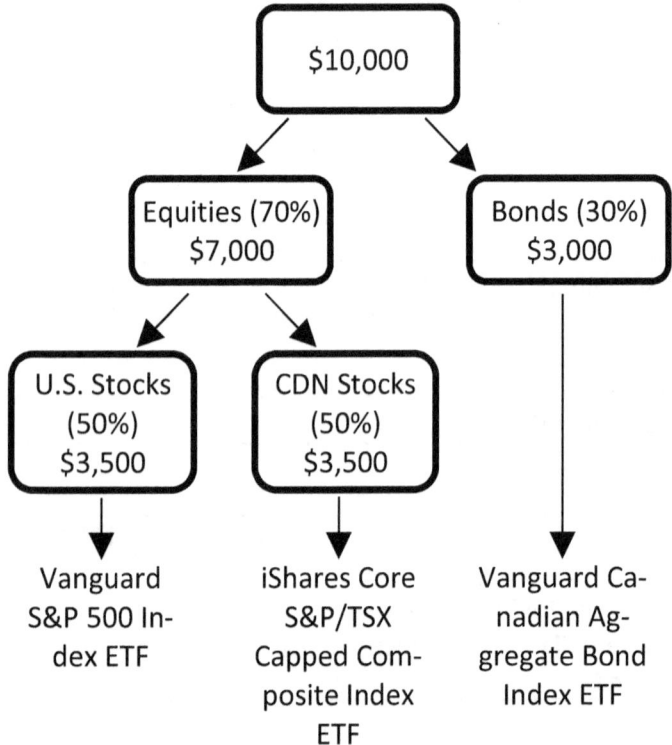

Designing and building your portfolio with ETFs is a lower cost
option to using mutual funds, but it is more time intensive and
requires establishing a discount brokerage account and paying
trading commissions and possibly account fees. It may also be
more difficult to take advantage of dollar-cost averaging due to
the difficulty of making regular contributions without paying
trading costs. For investors unwilling to pay the high MERs of
mutual funds, but not yet comfortable managing their own portfolio, an all-in-one portfolio may be right for you.

All-In-One Portfolio

For those of you who do not want to pay high MERs associated with mutual funds, but are not yet comfortable enough to manage your own portfolio, there exists a happy medium. Three of the most common platforms for younger Canadians are Tangerine, Wealthsimple and Questrade.

Tangerine

Tangerine offers mutual funds with an MER of 1.06%, which is lower than the industry average of about 2.5%. The account is free to set up and there is even an automatic savings program in which you can contribute as little as $25 a week directly from your bank account. At the time of writing, Tangerine offers five "Core Portfolios":

Balanced Income Portfolio
- 70% Canadian Bonds
- 10% Canadian Stocks
- 10% U.S. Stocks
- 10% International Stocks

Balanced Portfolio
- 40% Canadian Bonds
- 20% Canadian Stocks
- 20% U.S. Stocks
- 20% International Stocks

Balanced Growth Portfolio
- 25% Canadian Bonds
- 25% Canadian Stocks
- 25% U.S. Stocks
- 25% International Stocks

Equity Growth Portfolio
- 50% Canadian Stocks
- 25% U.S. Stocks
- 25% International Stocks

Dividend Portfolio
- 50% Canadian Dividend Equity
- 25% U.S. Dividend Equity
- 25% International Dividend Equity

Similarly, Tangerine also offers "Global ETF Portfolios" with even lower management and admin fees of 0.65%. At the time of writing, Tangerine offers three ETF-based portfolios:

Balanced ETF Portfolio
- 40% Bonds
- 60% Stocks

Equity Growth ETF Portfolio
- 100% Stocks

Balanced Growth ETF Portfolio
- 25% Bonds
- 75% Stocks

More information can be found at: www.tangerine.ca

Wealthsimple

Wealthsimple offers portfolio solutions with a free account set up and an automatic savings program in which you can also set up automatic contributions directly from your bank account. At the time writing, Wealthsimple offers various EFT-based portfolios based on investor risk tolerance such as "Conservative", "Balanced" and "Growth". The basic idea is the higher an investor's risk tolerance is, the more that particular portfolio will have exposure to stocks vs bonds and vice versa. The posted fees for those with less than 100,000 to invest are 0.50%. There are too many products available to list in this book, so for more information, please visit www.wealthsimple.com.

Questrade

Like Tangerine and Wealthsimple, Questrade also offers portfolio solutions with a free account set up and an automatic savings program in which you can also set up automatic contributions directly from your bank account. At the time writing, Questrade offers five ETF based "Questwealth Porfolios" with fees ranging from 0.11 % to 0.19%:

Aggressive Growth Portfolio
- 32% Canadian Stocks
- 32% U.S. Stocks
- 34% International Stocks
- <1 % Bonds
- 1% Cash

Growth Portfolio
- 26% Canadian Stocks
- 27% U.S. Stocks
- 27% International Stocks
- 18% Bonds
- 1% Cash

Balanced Portfolio
- 19% Canadian Stocks
- 20% U.S. Stocks
- 21% International Stocks
- 38% Bonds
- 1% Cash

Income Portfolio
- 13% Canadian Stocks
- 14% U.S. Stocks
- 13% International Stocks
- 58% Bonds
- 1% Cash

Conservative Income Portfolio
- 6% Canadian Stocks
- 7% U.S. Stocks
- 7% International Stocks
- 78% Bonds
- 1% Cash

More information can be found at: www.questrade.ca

The advantages of these portfolios are that they allow you to invest regularly into a portfolio by setting up the automatic savings program, pay lower fees than mutual funds and investment in a product that automatically rebalances. For the vast majority of readers, these portfolios provide an excellent starting point to begin investing.

No matter how you decide to start saving for your retirement, the most important thing you can do is to make a plan, start saving as early as possible and minimize fees. The most important investment you can make is to continue to educate yourself about personal finance.

CONCLUSION

I sincerely hope you enjoyed reading this book, but more importantly I hope you feel more empowered because of it. I hope that it fills some of the gaps in financial education that exists amongst most Canadian millennials.

In part 1, you gained an understanding of how the Canadian taxation system functions. You saw how investment income is taxed differently from employment income. In particular, income received from capital gains and dividends are taxed at a much lower rate than employment income.

In part 2, you learned about what federal government pensions are available to Canadians, when you can begin to receive them and how much you can expect to receive in retirement.

In part 3, I reviewed the two main registered savings vehicles available to Canadian millennials, the RRSP and TFSA. We examined what they are, who they benefit and which may be right for you.

In part 4, I introduced the different investment options available to you. We explored fixed income investment such savings accounts, and GICs and also equity investments such as stocks and income trusts. We then looked at the similarities and differences of mutual funds and their lower cost alternative ETFs.

In part 5, we looked at setting a goal, making a plan and taking action. We examined the benefits of making regular contributions to take advantage of dollar-cost averaging and introduced the concept of portfolio allocation. We then reviewed the different ways of making a plan such as working with a financial advisor, managing your own portfolio using ETFs and using an all-in-one portfolio.

With interest on savings at historical lows, the millennial investor will find it difficult to solely rely on savings accounts, or GICs. Explore in greater depth some of the topics covered in this book and look to stocks, trusts and ETFs as an essential part of your investment portfolio to generate satisfactory inflation-adjusted returns.

Relying on the CPP and OAS will not be sufficient to fund your retirement, and in the absence of a reliable workplace pension, you will have to take responsibility for your own financial future. Why? No one else will. Invest some time to further educate yourself on your investment options, then begin to make a plan and set savings and investment goals for yourself.

Always be aware of the fees that investment companies are charging, particularly mutual funds. These seemingly small fees can add up to significant amounts of money in the future.

The millennial generation has the advantage of time and the vast amount of free information to become empowered to make informed investments. These investments can compound over time to build tremendous wealth and provide an additional source of income in retirement.

For your financial empowerment,

Michael A. Pawlowsky

Twitter: @cdninvestor2000

Facebook: EMPOWERED MILLENNIAL INVESTOR

GLOSSARY

Part 1

Marginal (tax) Rate: The tax rate paid on one dollar of additional income.

Inflation: The tendency of the price of goods and services to increase over time.

Dividend: A payment made to a corporation's shareholders on a regular basis.

Capital Gain: A profit that is earned when you sell an asset for more than you paid for it.

Capital Loss: A financial loss that occurs when an investor sells an asset for less than they paid for it.

Part 4

Interest: The cost associated with borrowing money. It is paid to those lending money at a mutually agreed upon rate and interval for the duration of the loan.

Principal: The original amount of a fixed income investment.

Yield: The percentage of your investment that is paid to you as income on an annual basis.

Term: The amount of time that you must leave your money in a fixed income investment in order to receive your principal back.

<u>Maturity</u>: The end of the term of a fixed income investment in which the borrower has to pay back the full amount of the outstanding principal, plus any applicable interest to the lender.

<u>Stock</u>: A share of ownership in a corporation that investors buy and sell on stock exchanges. It is also known as share, common stock or equity.

<u>Market Capitalization</u>: "Market Cap" for short, is the total market value of a company's stock currently held by all of its shareholders.

<u>Mutual Fund</u>: A managed investment fund that pools money from many investors to purchase investments.

<u>Exchange Traded Fund (ETF)</u>: Similar to a mutual fund, but trades on a stock exchange and has a lower MER.

<u>Management Expense Ratio (MER)</u>: The costs associated with the management of an investment fund such as a mutual fund or ETF. It is expressed as a percentage of the fund's assets.

Part 5

<u>Dollar-Cost Averaging</u>: Making a regular fixed contribution to an investment to automate saving and buy more of an investment when it is low and less of it when it is high.

<u>Investment Portfolio</u>: The combination of various investment assets that an investor owns.

<u>Asset Allocation</u>: The mix of investments in an investment portfolio.

<u>Diversification</u>: A risk management strategy that reduces risk of investment loss in a portfolio by holding various types of investments.

About the Author

Michael A. Pawlowsky graduated with a Bachelor of Commerce from McGill University in Montreal and has over 20 years of investing experience. He seeks to empower a generation with the first step to become informed investors. He lives with his wife and son in Ottawa, Ontario.